LABYRINTH

An International Journal for Philosophy, Value Theory and Sociocultural Hermeneutics

Printed ISSN 2410-4817
Online ISSN 1561-8927

Vol. 19, No. 2, Winter 2017

NON-PHILOSOPHY, SOCIAL ACTION, AND PERFORMANCE: IN HONOR OF THE 80th ANNIVERSARY OF FRANÇOIS LARUELLE (Part 1)

Editor-in-Chief:
Prof. Dr. Yvanka B. Raynova

Managing Editor:
Dr. Susanne Moser

Advisory Board:

Prof. Dr. Seyla Benhabib (Boston), Prof. Dr. Debra Bergoffen (Fairfax), Prof. Dr. Peter Caws (Washington), Prof. Dr. Lester Embree (Florida), Prof. Dr. Reinhold Esterbauer (Graz), Prof. Dr. Nancy Fraser (New York), Dr. Ludger Hagedorn (Wien), Prof. Dr. Alison M. Jaggar (Boulder), Prof. Dr. Domenico Jervolino (Roma/Napoli), Prof. Dr. Andrzej M. Kaniowski (Łódź), Prof. Dr. Alexis Klimov † (Trois-Rivières), Prof. Dr. François Laruelle (Paris), Prof. Dr. Hedwig Meyer Wilmes (Nijmegen), Prof. Dr. Herta Nagl-Docekal (Wien), Prof. Dr. Elit Nikolov (Sofia), Prof. Dr. Sonja Rinofner-Kreidl (Graz), Prof. Dr. Hans-Walter Ruckenbauer (Graz), Prof. Dr. Ronald E. Santoni (Granville), Prof. Dr. Anne-Françoise Schmid (Paris), Prof. Dr. Hans-Reiner Sepp (Prague), Prof. Dr. Helmuth Vetter (Wien), Dr. Brigitte Weisshaupt (Zürich), Prof. Dr. Kurt Weisshaupt † (Zürich), Prof. Dr. Andrzej Wiercinski, Prof. Dr. Richard Wisser (Mainz)

Bibliographische Information der Deutschen Nationalbibliothek:
Die Deutsche Nationalbibliothek verzeichnet diese Publikation in der Deutschen
Nationalbibliographie, detaillierte bibliographische Daten sind im Internet unter
http://dnb.dnb.de aufrufbar.

Die wissenschaftliche und redaktionelle Arbeit wurde von der Kulturabteilung
der Stadt Wien – Wissenschafts- und Forschungsförderung unterstützt.

*Labyrinth: An International Journal for Philosophy, Value Theory and
Sociocultural Hermeneutics* is a serial publication of the Institut für Axiologische Forschungen / Institute for Axiological Research, Vienna – www.iaf.ac.at
For more information, please visit the Journal's homepage:
www.labyrinth.axiapublishers.com

© 2017 Axia Academic Publishers
Vienna
All Rights Reserved
Journal & Cover © 1999 Institut für Axiologische Forschungen
Printed in Germany

ISSN 2410-4817 / ISBN 978-3-903068-24-7

www.axiapublishers.com

LABYRINTH, Vol. 19, No. 2, Winter 2017

NON-PHILOSOHY, SOCIAL ACTION, AND PERFORMANCE

In Honor of the 80th Anniversary of François Laruelle (Part 1)

Table of Contents

EDITORIAL

Yvanka B. Raynova (Sofia/Vienna)
La "fête mobile" de la non-philosophie — 5

INTERVIEWS AND DIALOGUES

François Laruelle, Anne-Françoise Schmid (Paris)
A Mood for Philosophy — 14

Anthony Paul Smith (Philadelphia), Mark William Westmoreland (Villanova)
Harmonizing voices: François Laruelle and Anthony Paul Smith — 22

NON-PHILOSOPHY, SOCIAL ACTION, AND PERFORMANCE

Constance L. Mui (New Orleans), Julien S. Murphy (Portland, Maine)
Victims, Power and Intellectuals: Laruelle and Sartre — 35

Katerina Kolozova (Skopje)
Philosophy as capitalism and the socialist radically metaphysical response to it — 57

Adam Louis Klein (New York)
Peace between Trotskyism and Maoism: Non-Maoism and Double Superposition — 72

Nicholas Eppert (New York)
(Black) Non-Analysis: From the Restrained Unconscious
to the Generalized Unconscious — 86

Laura Cull Ó Maoilearca (Surrey)
From the Philosophy of Theatre to Performance Philosophy:
Laruelle, Badiou and the Equality of Thought — 102

Gilbert Kieffer (Santo Domingo/Kolsko)
La voix du philosophe Laruelle 121

Benoît Maire, Anne-Françoise Schmid (Paris)
Le sens-sans-signe: Pour une éthique de la création 132

Editorial

YVANKA B. RAYNOVA (Sofia/Vienne)

La "fête mobile" de la non-philosophie

The "moveable feast" of non-philosophy
(Abstract)

The editorial aims to unveil the attracting force of Laruelle's non-philosophy for scholars from different disciplines and even artists. It shows how a new "democratic order of thinking" permits non-philosophy to enclose domains that have long been considered as opposites: philosophy, science, religion and the arts. Conceived as parameters of thought of the same right and without privileges, these variables can be superposed in a process of creative invention. The performative force of non-standard thinking, which can take different forms of philo-fiction, science fiction, art fiction, Christo-Fiction etc., dismantles the decisional gestures and the sufficiency claims of philosophy, science and religion, and thus permits a regeneration as well as a choral orchestration in a "minimalistic symphony". In this sense, non-philosophy invites us every day to the "movable feast", that it is.

Keywords: François Laruelle, non-philosophy, philo-fiction, immanence, performance

Suivant une longue tradition un anniversaire est l'occasion d'une fête, surtout quand il s'agit d'un anniversaire à chiffre rond. Mais à part de cette tradition devenue habitude, est-ce qu'il y a toujours de quoi fêter? Dans le cas de François Laruelle il n'y en a pas une, mais plusieurs raisons de faire la fête. D'abord, peu de philosophes ont arrivé à l'âge de 80 ans. En France une telle chance avaient par exemple Levinas et Ricœur, mais pas Sartre, Merleau-Ponty, Foucault, Derrida ou Deleuze. C'est un vrai bonheur de voir devant nous un penseur si vivant et en bonne santé à un âge qui inspire le respect. Mais l'âge seul n'est pas dans ce cas ce qui donne le ton à la musique festive. C'est la personnalité de François et l'importance de son œuvre, par laquelle il est devenu ce qu'il "est", qui nous invitent à la fête.

Le mot *Festschrift* (volume commémoratif), qui est un mot composé de *Fest* (la fête) et de *Schrift* (l'écrit), convient parfaitement à cette occasion. J'ai eu l'idée de ce projet d'abord parce que je connaissais certaines œuvres de François que je trouvais fort originales – elles étaient pour moi comme un air frais dans une bibliothèque de vieux livres pleins de poussière. Il y a bien longtemps j'avais même traduit un article de lui en bulgare (cf. Laruelle 1991). Mais j'avoue que je n'avais aucune idée de l'impact de son œuvre, ni de l'ampleur de son influence. C'est pourquoi, après avoir lancé l'appel à contributions, j'ai étais très surprise de l'afflux de propositions d'articles. Les contributions que nous avons reçues étaient trop nombreuses pour être réunis dans une seule issue qui aurait eu environ 300 pages. Ainsi nous avons décidé d'abandonner un de nos projets prévus pour 2018 afin de publier la *Festschrift* en deux numéros conséquents.

Au cours du travail sur cette publication je me suis rendue compte qu'il y a une sorte de magnétisme dans la personne de François qui attire autant de jeunes chercheurs que de philosophes de courants différents et aussi – ce qui est assez rare – des artistes. On a raison donc de se demander en quoi consiste cette force d'attrait?

Gilbert Kieffer, pour qui François Laruelle est l'un des plus grands créateurs d'inventivité conceptuelle, décrit de la façon suivante la fascination qu'il découvre dans sa voix et dans son langage:

> … une voix qui se traduit elle-même, de neuf à chaque passage mélodique. Et ce n'est pas un leitmotiv, un thème récurrent. C'est une démarche qui procède par cercles concentriques, en spirale peut-être, depuis un motif reçu comme fictif, qui prolifère de manière fractale, en homothétie interne. (Kieffer 2017, 124)

Anne-Françoise Schmid nous fait part d'une chose semblable mais elle replace la figure des "cercles concentriques" par l'image picturale de la "ligne serpentine". Elle évoque l'enchantement de l'état d'esprit de création partagé pendant des décennies avec François qu'elle désigne par la notion de "mood" (Laruelle/Schmid 2017, 14-15). Rappelons que le mot anglais *mood* se traduit en allemand par *Stimmung,* une expression qui rend peut-être le mieux ce que Schmid et Kieffer décrivent, à savoir que la voix (*die Stimme*) du philosophe Laruelle crée une atmosphère très individuelle (*eine ganz eigene Stimmung*) qui permet en même temps un accord et un partage des voix entre les interlocuteurs (*Einstimmung und Stimmengleichheit*). Ainsi on pourrait dire dans un sens figuré que dans ce *mood/Stimmung* résonne tout le programme non-philosophique laruellien comme un accord "musical" entre l'Un et les multiplicités, comme une "fête mobile" – *a moveable feast,* pour utiliser le mot célèbre de Hemingway – du générique et du quantique. Pour exprimer la mobilité de la pensée non-philosophique ou non-standard Laruelle se sert du mot "flux":

> Ma manière de penser est plutôt de l'ordre du flux, je traverse les objets classiques de la philosophie sans me fixer sur eux. Ce qui m'intéresse, c'est le mouvement de la pensée, la flèche ou le vecteur... Il y a de grands thèmes dans mon évolution, mais traversés par un unique flux oscillant. Autrefois, je divisais ma production en stades (I, II, III, IV, V), mais j'y ai renoncé parce que j'en serais peut-être au VIIIe et cette succession n'aurait plus vraiment de sens. J'y ai renoncé, et je parlerais à présent plutôt de vagues qui se recouvrent les unes les autres. Des vagues qui se dirigent vers le même problème et traversent (se font à travers) une matière hétérogène. (Laruelle/ Forestier 2015).

Au lieu de tenter ici une impossible évocation de tous les "grands thèmes" laruelliens, tentons plutôt de nous immerger dans les profondeurs et l'origine de cet "unique flux oscillant", à savoir le principe clé de la non-philosophie. Ce principe ou code, c'est l'impératif de l'immanence radicale de l'Un par lequel Laruelle a suspendu et remplacé *la* question fondamentale (*die* Fundamentalfrage) de la philosophie (cf. Heidegger GA2, 6). Alors que les philosophies de l'immanence (Spinoza, Deleuze) ont posé l'immanence de façon transcendante, c'est-à-dire comme pensée *de* l'immanence qui pose celle-ci thétiquement, la radicalité de la non-philosophie exige de "traiter l'immanence de manière immanente" sans en faire un objet (Laruelle 2004a, 22). Cette immanence (à) soi, c'est ce que Laruelle appelle "l'Un-en-Un" (Laruelle 1996, 169), à savoir ce qui n'est trouvable précisément que dans l'Un et non à partir de l'Etre ou de l'Autre. Contrairement à la philosophie, qui en s'établissant dans l'Etre et l'Autre est devenue de plus en plus "oubli de l'essence de l'Un" (Laruelle 1989, 123; idem. 1992, 19; idem. 2004b), la non-philosophie part de cet impératif de l'immanence radicale de l'Un-en-Un. À première vue cette conception de l'Un peut apparaitre semblable à l'En-soi sartrien qui "est ce qu'il est", à savoir opaque et absolument identique à soi-même (Sartre 1943, 34). Mais précisément, l'En-soi sartrien renvoie à la question sur l'Être, il est un concept ontologique fondamental d'une philosophie qui est par excellence décision et scission, opérant par dualités d'opposition tel que "être – néant", "en-soi – pour-soi", "pour-soi – pour-l'autre", "être – phénomène" etc. Par contre, étant en-Un, l'Un laruellien est "sans-consistance ontologique, langagière ou mondaine, sans-être ou sans-essence, sans-langage et sans-pensée, même s'il se dit de cette manière avec l'aide de l'Etre, du langage, de la pensée, etc." (Laruelle 1996, 34). Pour le non-philosophe il ne s'agit pas de *penser l'Un* mais de penser *selon l'Un*, qui tout en restant immanent en lui-même est la condition préalable de toute pensée et respectivement de toute philosophie, de toute science, de toute pensée de l'art ou de la religion. De cette façon on arrive à une "vision-en-Un" qui n'est plus la pensée-connaissance de la philosophie classique qui reflète ou redouble le Réel – la perception, la représentation, l'intuition, la réflexion etc. –, mais une pensée sans pensée, non-intuitive, non-conceptuelle, un donner "sans-donation", un clonage transcendantal (clonage et donc pas coupure en deux!), qui est "déterminé-en-dernière-instance par le Réel inaliénable.

Or, la vision-en-Un recèle d'une "dualité unilatérale" (Laruelle 1992, 126), qui étant identique a un seul côté et non pas deux: le Réel n'est pas un côté, il est la condition, l'origine et l'avènement de la multiplicité de façon unilatérale et irréversible, tandis que la multiplicité est analogue au Réel/l'Un par son identité ou intégration (Laruelle 1996, 36). Autrement dit, comme unilatérale la "vision-en-Un" suit la distinction différentielle transcendantale, tandis que comme dualité elle suit l'intégration analogique. Par conséquence le Sujet transcendantal, qui est le seul côté ici, est sous-déterminé en-dernière-instance par le Réel/Un caractérisé par son immanence. Le Sujet est à la fois inhérent à cette immanence qui fait la Dernière Instance et hétérogène par rapport à elle ou en état de se rapporter à l'expérience depuis l'intérieur de cette dernière instance (Laruelle 2010).

L'Un/le Réel, qui ne peut donc pas être connu par apperception empirique ou transcendantale, ni par réflexion ou synthèse, ni réduit au "monde" ou à une matière première, reste une énigme. De ce fait l'Un ne peut pas être l'objet d'une phénoménologie ou d'une herméneutique. Mais comme *Ereignis* effectuant la multiplicité il peut être décrit et interprété par ses effets ou (re)modelé par le matériel que nous offrent les philosophies, les sciences, les arts et les religions, en proposant un mode de penser uni-latéralisant. Laruelle parle en ce sens d'"un usage d'abstraction axiomatique" des termes philosophiques (Laruelle 1996, 36) et plus récemment de "complémentarité unilatérale de l'axiomatique et de l'herméneutique" (Laruelle, 2008b). L'applicabilité de ce procédé de la non-philosophie est articulé dans la définition même de la non-philosophie comme "un usage unique ou une pensée transcendantale pour la philosophie et identiquement la science, l'éthique, l'art, ou pour toute autre région d'objet" (Laruelle 1996, 22). En quoi consiste cette applicabilité unique?

Un trait original de la non-philosophie est le fait qu'elle nous permet de prendre n'importe quelle philosophie ou discipline comme matériel et de lui ajouter un facteur X, c'est-à-dire d'en appliquer la formule de la matrice générique, qui consiste dans l'unité de la science, de la philosophie et du sujet sous la science (Laruelle 2008b). En universalisant et ramenant ainsi ce matériel philosophique à sa détermination-en-dernière-instance (DDI) on enlève son (auto)suffisance et le transforme en non-X: en non-marxisme, non-éthique, non-esthétique etc. Cette universalisation peut à premier abord paraitre semblable à la méthode de réduction transcendantale et eidétique de Husserl qui a pour but de faire ressortir les structures universelles d'un phénomène donné que serait dans ce cas une philosophie particulière. Mais une telle analogie serait apparente, car il s'agit d'un "usage générique" dégageant les invariants génériques des axiomes philosophiques pour les reconduire à l'immanence. Les procédés qu'utilise Laruelle sous le nom de "science générique" sont inspiré par la physique quantique et sont d'une extrême complexité (cf. ibid.). Dans une de ses lettres il l'explique de la façon suivante:

> … le générique est un facteur=X qui s'ajoute à un savoir ou un produit déjà existant dans lequel il intervient, sans le nier ou le détruire, pour le libérer d'une limitation, changer de destination sa puissance et l'orienter en fonction de son adéquation à l'homme ou au "sujet". Une telle transformation qui ne détruit pas un savoir mais en ré-oriente la destination en fonction du sujet, certains l'appellent une « vérité ». Pour notre part nous dirons un « mal minimal » qui puisse être immédiatement un bien positif, le seul bien qui ne soit donc pas vicieux et ne se retourne pas en un mal. Lorsqu'il s'agit comme ici du pouvoir philosophique, il est de lever la suffisance ou l'abus d'origine transcendantal sur le réel. Le générique ne s'oppose pas au philosophique, il s'en émancipe ou s'en libère par un mal minimal. (…)
>
> (…) De quoi le quantique est-il ici le modèle? Une telle constante, réelle mais non spécialement physique et quantifiable, est par un côté immanence mais comprise comme addition idempotente (c'est la constante d'esprit quantique, opposée au Tout transcendant ou omnipotent). Par son autre côté, elle est transcendance de type philosophique, mais dont les deux côtés (…) sont réduits à un seul comme interférence. (…) Le côté de transcendance unilatérale est lui aussi idempotent et ne détruit pas l'immanence qui, elle, transforme la transcendance. L'addition idempotente $1+1=1$, le propre de l'immanence qui ne change pas, modifie ou "transforme" la transcendance qu'elle reçoit et dont elle a besoin pour passer d'idempotente à générique et devenir $1+1=11/2$. Cette propriété de l'addition générique qui ne change rien aux sciences et aux philosophies sauf leur destination ou leur "transformation", est l'excès que nous cherchions. (Laruelle 2008a)

Les livres de Laruelle nous offrent des applications diverses de ce modèle ou procédé tout en inspirant les chercheurs d'en faire leur propres expériences et applications. Un bon exemple en ce sens est l'*Introduction au Non-Marxisme* (cf. Laruelle 2000), qui propose une axiomatisation transcendantale du marxisme et le défait de ses postulats philosophiques, notamment historico-dialectiques, pour l'universaliser. Laruelle y montre l'insuffisance de la détermination-en-dernière-instance marxiste et la nécessité de la replacer par une version plus radicale, ainsi que par un style non-philosophique qui met en jeu la dualité uni-latérale, l'universel, l'Autre-sans-altérité, le vrai-sans-vérité etc. Cela lui permet de faire ressortir certains aspects restés voilés ou impensés autant dans la philosophie de Marx que dans ses réceptions. Katerina Kolozova qui adopte en partie ce style pour ses propres analyses remarque:

> The analogy of superposition taken from Laruelle's non-standard philosophy (...), and inspired by quantum theory, serves to enable us to understand the fundamentally social nature of the individual and its reverse, not as a paradox but as two realities that can be viewed unilaterally. The fact that they are viewed unilaterally does not mean that one does not affect the other as its real foregrounding and its determination in the last instance. (...) What matters is that the social constitutes a real in its own right, as does the human-in-human, and that one conditions the other by immanently affecting it. (Kolozova 2017, 69-70)

En même temps elle met en garde contre une superposition qui serait un projet spéculatif purement autoréférentiel et sans relevance pour l'édification d'une société d'égalité et de bien-être pour chacun (ibid.).

L'efficacité de la méthode laruellienne de superposition est démontrée dans l'article d'Adam Klein "Peace between Trotskyism and Maoism: Non-Maoism and Double Superposition" (Klein 2017) par une démarche novatrice. Klein y propose une application radicalisée de la dualyse par double superposition dans le but de purger le Maoisme et le Trotskysme de leurs dogmatismes et de les mettre en paix. Pour cela il effectue deux clones non-philosophiques. Il transforme d'abord le Trotskysme en l'isolant de sa structure philosophique auto-positionnelle et ensuite il utilise ce Trotskysme radicalisé pour transformer le Maoisme. Le résultat de cette expérimentation fictionnelle est un Maoisme-Trotskysme radicalisé qui ouvre une nouvelle perspective pour l'intégration de ces deux modes de pensée opposés et la paix.

Dans sa *Théorie des étrangers* (Laruelle 1998) Laruelle propose une autre application de l'axiomatique non-philosophique qui révise radicalement la psychanalyse et la science dite "de l'homme". Contre la philosophie et la psychanalyse il y démontre que l'homme n'est pas "sujet", "conscience" ou "inconscient", mais une identité de moi-en-moi ou d'ego-en-ego. En même temps la dualité unilatérale dévoile l'homme aussi comme "humanité" et par-là comme Etranger. Il s'ensuit que le Moi et l'Etranger sont identiques en-dernière-instance, une découverte qui ouvre le champ d'une nouvelle théorie unifiée ou science générique à partir de l'Un/Réel qu'est l'Homme en tant qu'Etranger. Cette théorie parait particulièrement féconde dans le domaine des recherches analytiques.

Ainsi, dans son article "Blackness that is 'Lived-without-Life'" (Eppert 2017), Nicholas Eppert montre comment on peut utiliser la théorie laruellienne de l'homme pour ce qu'il appelle "(Black) Non-Analysis". Du fait que l'inconscient restreint de l'homme blanc est selon Laruelle une "demi perte", il s'en suit que l'inconscient généralisé de l'homme noir ne peut pas y apparaitre puisqu'il est une "perte absolue". L'ouverture de l'inconscient restreint de l'homme blanc à l'inconscient généralisé de l'homme noir, qui est son identité en-dernière-instance, ne peut être effectué que par le désir de "mettre fin au monde". La tâche du non-analyste (noir) serait alors de capturer ce désir de l'inconscient restreint de l'homme blanc par une dualyse à partir de l'Un.

Rappelons que Laruelle a poussé sa théorie de l'Etranger plus loin sous la forme de science ou gnose hérétique dans ses livres ultérieurs *Le Christ futur: Une leçon d'hérésie* (Laruelle 2002), qui dévoile l'Homme-en-personne dans son essence de Christ futur, et *Christo-fiction: Les ruines d'Athènes et de Jérusalem* (Laruelle 2014), qui apporte à l'Homme un nouveau message de salut. Ces lectures a-religieuses du judaïsme et du christianisme sont très importantes à un double titre. Elles représentent d'une part une nouvelle alternative aux recherches contemporaines atheistes, non-theistes et scientifiques tel que "New Atheism" (Dawkins, Hitchens, Harris, Dennett), "Anatheism" (Kearney), "Religion without God" (Dworkin), "After God" (Taylor, Sloterdijk), "Religious Naturalism" (Wieman, Stone, Rue, Crosby, Goodenough), "Dieu à venir" (Meillassoux) etc. D'autre part elles ont inspiré des interprétations hérétiques non-religieuses, en particulier le "non-bouddhisme spéculatif" de Glenn Wallis, qui a repris les concepts laruelliens de "décision", d'"auto-position", de "spécularité" et d'"immanence radicale" (Wallis 2013, 225).

De toutes les applications de la non-philosophie ou philosophie non-standard la plus intéressante est peut-être la philo-fiction – un genre parallèle à la science-fiction, qui opère "un abaissement de la dogmatique et de l'axiomatique philosophique à l'état de fiction" (Laruelle 2015, 82). Le renouvellement non-standard de la fiction rend possible la rencontre et la réunion de domaines qui ont été longtemps considéré comme opposés – la philosophie, les sciences, la religion et les arts – dans un "nouvel ordre démocratique" (Laruelle 1996, 16). Conçu comme des paramètres de la pensée du même droit et sans privilèges, si ce n'est la scientificité même, ces variables peuvent être superposés ou noués dans un procès d'invention, de réinvention et/ou de clonage. La force performative de la pensée non-standard, qui peut prendre des formes différentes – philo-fiction, science-fiction, art-fiction, Christo-Fiction –, démonte la décision et avec elle toutes prétentions de suffisance provenant non seulement de la philosophie, mais aussi des sciences et des religions. Cela devient possible grâce aux principes et les instruments nouveaux de la non-philosophie laruellienne mentionnés, qui servent de base pour une meilleure compréhension des domaines en question, ainsi que pour leur régénération.

Le peintre Benoît Maire explique qu'au début de ses études la philosophie et l'art étaient pour lui comme la peinture et son cadre: l'art prenait son expression d'une source inconnue tandis que la philosophie l'analysait en se construisant autour comme une coquille. Mais par ses travaux avec Anne-Françoise Schmid et l'accès à la non-philosophie il s'est rendu compte que la philosophie n'est pas un parergon de l'activité artistique étant elle-même aussi libre et créative que l'art (Maire 2017, 170). Or la représentation de la philosophie comme "cadre" dans l'intuition initiale de Maire n'est ni fortuite, ni complètement fausse. Le cadre ou l'encadrement, c'est précisément ce que Laruelle appelle le "principe de suffisance", c'est-à-dire la façon de la philosophie – ou du moins de certaines doctrines philosophiques – de s'auto-donner une autorité qui bloque l'accès à l'usage de son propre discours, une autorité de système qui prétend de fournir une vérité éternelle, absolue et exclusive. La philo-fiction, par contre, est un mouvement d'invention qui refuse tout despotisme (cf. Laruelle/Forestier 2015). C'est pour cela que des théoricien(ne)s de la performativité et du théâtre, comme p.ex. Laura Cull, s'emparent du style laruellien pour dénoncer les gestes autoritaires de certains philosophes qui ont tendance à se mettre dans le rôle d'autorités intitulés à déterminer les critères de ce qu'est le théâtre et à juger quelles pratiques d'art sont meilleures ou pires (Cull 2017).

Tout en critiquant certaines pratiques philosophiques, la pensée non-standard reconnait le droit d'être des philosophies différentes qu'elle cherche à radicaliser par son "non" hérétique et à réintégrer dans une nouvelle composition. Ainsi remodelées elles forment une œuvre chorale (Laruelle 2017), une symphonie minimaliste, épurée du superflu. Et cela nous rappelle que la vraie fête ne commence pas nécessairement avec un anniversaire, mais avec l'émancipation du fardeau du quotidien et la joie du partage des cadeaux spirituels. En ce sens la non-philosophie nous invite chaque jour à la fête qu'elle est elle-même.

Prof. Dr. Yvanka B. Raynova, Institute for the Study of Societies and Knowledge – Bulgarian Academy of Sciences, Sofia / Institut für Axiologische Forschungen, Wien,
raynova[at]iaf.ac.at

References

Cull Ó Maoilearca, Laura. "Equalizing Theatre and Philosophy: Laruelle, Badiou, and gestures of authority in the philosophy of theatre," *Performance Philosophy*, Vol. 3, No. 3 (2017): 730-750.

Eppert, Nicholas. "(Black) Non-Analysis: From the Restrained Unconscious to the Generalized Unconscious", *Labyrinth: An International Journal for Philosphy, Vaule Theory and Sociocultural Hermeneutics*, Vol. 19, No. 2 (2017): 87-102.

Heidegger, Martin. *Sein und Zeit* (GA Bd. 2). Frankfurt am Main: Vittorio Klostermann, 1977.

Kieffer, Gilbert. "La voix du philosophe François Laruelle", *Labyrinth: An International Journal for Philosphy, Vaule Theory and Sociocultural Hermeneutics*, Vol. 19, No. 2 (2017): 122-132.

Klein, Adam. "Peace between Trotskyism and Maoism: Non-Maoism and Double Superposition," *Labyrinth: An International Journal for Philosphy, Vaule Theory and Sociocultural Hermeneutics*, Vol. 19, No. 2 (2017): 72-86.

Kolozova, Katerina. "Philosophy as Capitalism and the Socialist Radically Metaphysical Response to it,"*Labyrinth: An International Journal for Philosphy, Vaule Theory and Sociocultural Hermeneutics*, Vol. 19, No. 2 (2017): 57-71.

Maire, Benoît. "Philosophy and Art", *Aleï Journal #2* (2017): 166-174.

Laruelle, François. "Le point sur l'Un", in Stamelman, Richard Howard et Mary Ann Caws (eds.). *Ecrire le livre: autour d'Edmond Jabès. Colloque de Cerisy-la-Salle*. Seyssel: Editions Chap Vallon, 1989, 121-132.

Laruelle, François. "Razlichie i tujdestvo: budesteto na misulta" (Différence et identité: l'avenir de la pensée). *Filosofska misul*, No. 1 (1991): 101-113.

Laruelle, François. *Théorie des identités*. Paris: PUF, 1992.

Laruelle, François. *Principes de la non-philosophie*. Paris: PUF, 1996.

Laruelle, François. *Introduction au Non-Marxisme*. Paris: PUF, 2000.

Laruelle, François. *Le Christ future: une leçon d'hérésie*. Paris: Exils, 2002.

Laruelle, François. *La Lutte et l'Utopie à la fin des temps philosophiques* (LU), 2004a.

Laruelle, François. "Nouvelle présentation de la non-philosophie", *Organisation Non-Philosophique Internationale*, 02.11.2004b. Web. <http://www.onphi.net/corpus/31/nouvelle-presentation-de-la-non-philosophie>.

Laruelle, François. "Enfin le fondement générique d'une science de la philosophie", *Organisation Non-Philosophique Internationale*, 9 février, 2008a. Web. <http://www.onphi.net/letters/21/enfin-le-fondement-generique-d-une-science-de-la-philosophie>.

Laruelle, François. "Quelle science est la non-philosophie?" *Organisation Non-Philosophique Internationale*, 5 novembre, 2008b. Web. <https://www.onphi.net/letters/86/quelle-science-est-la-non-philosophie->.

Laruelle, François. "Le code non-philosophique", *Organisation Non-Philosophique Internationale*, 6 février, 2010. Web. <https://www.onphi.net/letters/99/le-code-non-philosophique >.

Laruelle, François. *Christo-fiction: Les ruines d'Athènes et de Jérusalem*. Paris: Fayard, 2014.

Laruelle, François et Florian Forestier. "Entretien avec François Laruelle : Autour de Christo-fiction", *Actu-Philosophia*, 17 janvier, 2015. Web. <http://www.actu-philosophia.com/Entretien-avec-Francois-Laruelle-Autour-de>.

Laruelle, François et Anne-Françoise Schmid. "A Mood for Philosophy", *Labyrinth: An International Journal for Philosphy, Vaule Theory and Sociocultural Hermeneutics*, Vol. 19, No. 2 (2017):14-21.

Sartre, Jean-Paul. *L'être et le néant*. Paris: Gallimard, 1943.

Wallis, Glenn. "Nascent Speculative Non-Buddhism", *Journal for the Study of Religions and Ideologies*, Vol. 12, issue 35 (Summer 2013): 222-247.

INTERVEWS & DIALOGUES

FRANÇOIS LARUELLE, ANNE-FRANÇOISE SCHMID (Paris)

A Mood for Philosophy

A mood for Philosophy
(Abstract)

In this dialogue with Francois Laruelle Anne-Françoise Schmid suggests that Laruelle's non-philosophy, which begins with an indecision, could be conceived as something that in the history of painting has been called figura serpentinata, "serpentine line". This line, which produces a kind of music by the use of concepts, is visible according her trough his whole work: from his first book on Ravaisson, Phenomenon and Difference (1971), *through to his last one,* The Last Humanity: A New Ecological Science, *published in French in 2015 and expected to appear in English in 2018.*

Keywords: Non-philosophy, the One, the generic, quantum physics, transcendental, transcendence

Introduction au dialogue

J'aime le terme de mood, qui me vient de la traduction en anglais du titre d'un très beau film chinois : *A Mood for Love*. Que serait un *mood for philosophy*? Cette affect si particulier, atmosphère, *Stimmung*, émotion, probablement proche de ce que l'on peut vivre en jouant ensemble de la musique?

J'aimerais suggérer ici que ce "Mood" est ce qui rend possible la vie quotidienne et commune de deux humains en tant que philosophes, engagés dans la création plutôt que dans la consommation. François a vécu la moitié de sa vie avec moi, et moi les deux tiers de la mienne avec lui.

C'est dans cette atmosphère, partageant le même bureau, que se construit à la fois autonomie et concertation implicites. Il y a des concepts partout, qui passent évidemment de l'un à l'autre, concepts le plus souvent rendus autonomes des autres philosophes, dont le nom apparaît dans nos échanges plutôt comme nom de théorèmes que de philosophies. Et, lorsque, par grâce, un nouveau concept apparaît, il n'y a jamais de critique, jamais de limitation empirique. C'est comme cela, il est là, il trouvera sa place par son mouvement.

Sans ce "philosophical mood", la vie du couple philosophique serait entrecoupée de remarques, de reprises. Il y aurait des discussions ou des disputes que nous avons toujours jugées inutiles. Pourrait-on les surmonter par l'humour? Freud a montré que l'humour est un triomphe du moi. Non, il y a des continuités mobiles, des trajectoires à la fois naturelles et surprenantes qui ont des effets corrélatifs dans les vécus philosophiques, sans que l'on sache exactement où ni comment.

J'aimerais manifester ces trajectoires grâce une analogie. Je pense au Moïse de Michel-Ange dans l'abbatiale de Saint-Pierre aux liens à Rome, pour le mausolée du pape Jules II, sur lequel il existe un beau texte de Freud. Si on regarde longtemps Moïse, on s'aperçoit qu'il n'est pas possible de décider s'il se lève pour manifester sa colère contre les Juifs adorant le veau d'or ou s'il s'assied de désespérance, pensant qu'il n'y a plus rien à faire, alors qu'il tient sous son bras droit les tables de la loi qu'il vient de recevoir de Jehova. Cette indécidabilité en art et en philosophie a un nom, elle s'appelle "ligne serpentine", ce qu'on appelle à l'époque de Michel-Ange une *figura serpentinata* (Careri 2013, 29-30), qui avait un sens aussi bien artistique que théologique, la serpentine christique. Par la ligne serpentine, on monte au paradis, on est jeté aux enfers et l'artiste peut animer un tableau ou une fresque, comme Michel-Ange celle de la Chapelle sixtine, dite "Le Jugement dernier".

Cette ligne serpentine, François l'a faite revivre en philosophie dans son premier ouvrage publié, *Phénomène et Différence. Essai sur Ravaisson* (Laruelle 1971). On la retrouve partout, dans toute son œuvre, et elle est la dynamique de son dernier ouvrage : *En dernière humanité. La nouvelle science écologique* (Laruelle 2015), où l'écologie, habituellement réduite aux mouvements horizontaux de la planète, trouve sa dimension verticale. François cite de temps en temps "La charrue et les étoiles", du poète irlandais Sean O'Casey, manière de nous rappeler qu'il est fils de paysan devenu philosophe et titre qu'il transforme en "De la caverne aux étoiles", selon la ligne serpentine.

Cette ligne serpentine, comme je le suggérais, est une condition de notre vie commune en tant que philosophes. Mais elle est plus, elle produit une sorte de musique, "faire de la musique avec des concepts", c'est d'ailleurs ce que lui avait dit Clémence Ramnoux lors de sa soutenance de thèse, "vous avez voulu faire de la musique avec des concepts", formule qu'il revendique toujours, et que vous allez retrouver dans sa conférence. C'est l'objet de cette journée, où François présentera son dernier ouvrage, sa tétralogie sur la philosophie et la musique. La ligne serpentine fait donc aussi résonner la philosophie. Et pourtant Freud, dans son article sur le Moïse, se déclare insensible à la musique. Montrons que nous pouvons y être plus que sensibles sans avoir besoin de tourner autour d'elle, comme autour d'une sculpture ! Peut-être la philosophie permet-elle de sculpter à sa façon la musique.

Anne-Françoise Schmid

François Laruelle en dialogue avec Anne-Françoise Schmid[1]

Schmid: Je commence par l'idée qui est toujours la mienne mais qui a toujours été quelque chose de notre lien. Lorsque nous nous sommes rencontrés, tu travaillais déjà sur plusieurs philosophies, Nietzsche, Heidegger, Marx et aussi Deleuze et Derrida. Il y a toujours eu chez toi une intrication de plusieurs philosophies dans ton travail, ce que tu appelles maintenant un "chaos-gito". Or je suis persuadée qu'on devint philosophe non pas en en lisant un seul en passant, mais en étant capable de construire un pont entre des philosophies qui ne sont pas spécialement faites pour se rencontrer. Et là, avec toi, je trouvais justement quelque chose comme cela. Il y avait un philosophe. Et derrière chaque philosophe, quelque chose de toute la philosophie. J'avais moi-même, adolescente, fait des travaux sur Descartes et Leibniz en même temps, pas seulement Descartes, ou Leibniz, ou Malebranche. Quelque chose qui relie et sépare chacune de ces philosophies, ne sachant pas si on a là la philosophie ou les philosophies, mais je pensais que l'idéal, c'était la communication des deux. Et avec toi, je trouvais quelqu'un qui avait modifié la façon de compter sans se vouer à l'histoire de la philosophie, une, deux, trois philosophies, quel sens est-ce que cela a? Aucun immédiatement. Mais tu avais trouvé l'Un, puis le deux, puis trois, puis le quatre, chaque fois comme un recommencement. Tu as fondé comme cela une non-philosophie moderne, un "non-" inventif, non pas restrictif, puis la philosophie non-

---

[1] A partir d'un enregistrement fait le 20 octobre 2017 à Kolsko, Pologne, par Gilbert et Anetka Kieffer.

standard quand il articule une nouvelle multiplicité dite "quantique", et maintenant, tu revendiques de nouveau quelque chose comme la philosophie dans son compagnonnage avec la musique, c'est une nouvelle façon de compter les philosophies, sans abandonner la non-philosophie et le non-standard. L'ensemble est extraordinairement inventif. Moi ce que je fais dans cet horizon, c'est ajouter des axiomes intermédiaires pour faire le passage entre l'Un et les multiplicités.

Laruelle: C'est ce que j'appelle maintenant une sorte de regard en arrière, une symphonie de philosophies, ou un chœur de philosophes. La philosophie c'est un grand chœur.

Schmid: Une affaire chorale. C'est une première transformation musicale. Est-ce que tu y entends des voix graves et des voies aiguës?

Laruelle: Oui, la quantique c'est plutôt une voix grave, de baryton, le générique, l'autre côté, l'autre face de la chose, peut-être de ténor, voire plus aiguë en tout cas, et la philosophie au milieu. C'est peut-être elle qui est la voix de baryton, la voix synthétique par rapport aux deux voix extrêmes. Enfin, on peut l'imaginer comme cela. Évidemment, c'est une image, une image certes, mais c'est tout mon problème, comment passer de la sonorité conceptuelle à la sonorité musicale. Je traite la philosophie de "belle insonore".

Schmid: Une voix synthétique? Tu penses que l'on fabrique les philosophies?

Laruelle: Plutôt que fabriquer de la philosophie, on fabrique des philosophes.

Schmid: Toujours au pluriel.

Laruelle: Oui, toujours au pluriel. Moi, maintenant, je vis dans un système de philosophies au pluriel. Je ne peux pas me représenter comme dépendant uniquement d'un seul philosophe comme cela se fait dans l'université et dans le travail universitaire.

Schmid: Quand tu as créé la non-philosophie, tu as eu un moment où il a fallu te distancier des philosophies. Et au fond, j'aimais cette idée de multiple que tu regardais avec une certaine distance.

Laruelle: Et une certaine méfiance.

Schmid: Et une certaine méfiance, pensant que cela retombait dans la philosophie, ce qui partiellement était vrai, bien entendu. Mais néanmoins maintenant tu récupères la multiplicité des philosophies dans ton idée de "composition philo-musicale".

Laruelle: J'ai beaucoup travaillé l'idée d'un retrait philosophique, pas d'absence, oui, mais d'un retrait, une certaine distance par rapport aux grandes ambitions classiques de la philosophie, mais ce retrait était fait pour se terminer par une avancée, par un sursaut en quelque sorte, la philosophie gagnait sa plus grande vigueur lorsqu'elle prenait un recul par rapport à elle-même et qu'elle pouvait se relancer et s'amplifier. Maintenant je vais un peu sur ce schème que j'applique à la fois au générique mais surtout aux philosophies, au statut des philosophies.

Schmid: Le geste classique, c'est de définir la philosophie indirectement par d'autres disciplines, ce n'est pas de la technologie, ce n'est pas des sciences, ce n'est pas de l'esthétique, ce n'est pas de l'art, etc., mais cela a à voir avec chacune d'entre elles. Mais toi tu fais autre chose qui est tout à fait nouveau, c'est que d'une certaine façon tu opères une fusion de la musique et de la philosophie par l'idée de composition, et tu transformes les concepts de la philosophie pour la mettre au diapason de l'art. A mon avis, tu représentes toi-même une multiplicité entre la tradition, dont tu fais usage comme d'un matériau, la non-philosophie, puis le "non-" déplacé d'un non-standard, et puis maintenant, philosophie et musique, composées ou intriquées. Ce sont des passages que tu désignes des "vagues" différentes, ce qui rend la philosophie magnifique comme la mer.

Laruelle: Il y a toujours eu une triplicité de la structure de la philosophie. Ici, la philosophie se tient au centre autonome de l'appareil, entre d'une part le quantique qui lui sert de base ou de fondement, la philosophie, étant l'axe transcendantal, et de l'autre côté, le philosophique investi dans l'expérience serait le générique. Je récupère le thème du générique et le thème du quantique par le moyen ou à travers le philosophique. J'ai un petit embarras surtout actuellement pour situer exactement la musique, que je veux absolument restituer physiquement, parce que c'est fondamental pour mon projet. J'aurais tendance à lui donner la place du générique, c'est-à-dire à relayer celui-ci, qui est la structure de l'expérience humaine, par la musique. C'est au fond la musique qui nous introduit le plus radicalement à l'expérience. C'est l'art en général évidemment pour étendre les choses, mais la musique est le vécu le plus direct vers l'expérience et ses performances spontanées. J'hésite un peu sur la place de la musique entre le générique et le philosophique, mais c'est plutôt du côté du générique. Je finirai par lui trouver la meilleure place.

Schmid: De mon côté, sur mon terrain des institutions scientifiques, j'ai beaucoup utilisé ces concepts pour comprendre ce qu'il se passait dans l'invention scientifique et son usage, et la tripartition quantique, générique, philosophique est véritablement très utile. Maintenant, dans les régimes interdisciplinaires, on a besoin d'une musique à fonction générique dans les sciences. Le quantique amène de son côté quelque chose des méthodes récentes dans la science fondamentale, et la philosophie devient une pièce d'articulation dans les sciences elles-mêmes, mais sans l'interprétation métaphysique généralisante. Le quantique et le générique empêchent cela. Ce qui est extraordinaire dans cette structure, c'est qu'elle est adaptable aussi bien en sciences que dans les arts, et dans la philosophie elle-même. Du point de vue de la simple philosophie, tu peux décomposer en elle quelque chose qui lui sert de point d'extériorité par exemple, chez Kant, la mécanique, chez Platon la politique, tu peux les en sortir, les défaire entre générique et quantique, et réinterpréter ces philosophies avec une sorte de liberté, qu'eux-mêmes ne pouvaient pas exercer, parce que ces choses-là étaient comme dans le cœur de leur système.

Laruelle: Trop fixées.

Schmid: Trop fixées. La mécanique était trop importante d'une certaine façon chez Kant. Et d'ailleurs Kant a fait des découvertes scientifiques, il ne faut pas oublier qu'il est, avec Laplace, à l'origine de la théorie scientifique des nébuleuses. Dans cette dé-fixation, comment peut se discerner le futur de la philosophie? Comment introduire du futur cette structure? La philosophie se continue toujours, mais on peut toujours la manifester en fonction de cette tripartition. Ce qui est terminé, c'est le survol de la philosophie sur les autres disciplines, qui "boucle" les sciences et les autres productions humaines. Car tant que la philosophie a survolé les sciences, c'était bouclé. La philosophie, c'était une théorie qui avait des concepts et de l'expérience, et c'était bloqué dans cette organisation. Pas d'ouverture. Avec le générique et le quantique, on a une ouverture, on fait voir des ingrédients scientifiques très différents.

Laruelle: Les anciens excès de la philosophie lui sont maintenant interdits par les disciplines qui lui servent de contrefort.

Schmid: Elle leur est accolée, mais elle est active et dynamique. Avec l'hétérogénéité du générique et du quantique, elle trouve une dynamique qu'elle n'avait pas dans sa stricte affirmation de soi. Et c'est la même chose concernant les arts, elle retrouve une dynamique devant l'hétérogénéité, en lui donnant un statut. La philosophie n'est pas plus importante que les mathématiques. Les mathématiques doivent revoir aussi complètement leur place. On doit réinterpréter cette place qui n'est plus celle d'un langage universel, mais peut être articulée à toute autre discipline ou activité humaine.

Laruelle: Enfin, la philosophie est quand même la plus importante en un sens pour moi, évidemment, ce n'est pas la philosophie au sens classique. La philosophie c'est l'axe ou la flèche de la cathédrale pour moi. C'est l'acte de transcendance, et c'est la flèche qui monte vers le ciel mais qui est aussi inversée, qui peut très bien descendre du ciel vers la terre, car le transcendantal a deux sens, il est inversable.

Schmid: Ce que tu as ajouté dans la philosophie, avec d'autres, mais c'est toi qui l'a fait de la façon la plus radicale, c'est la dimension verticale. Levinas avait tenté de le faire avec l'éthique, la dimension verticale. Mais je pense que ton livre *En dernière humanité* est le premier essai où, dans l'écologie, qui est en fait pour nous une grande surface horizontale ou une sorte d'anneau autour de la Terre, a été ajouté un axe vertical. Et là, je crois que tu es le premier. Et cette idée de flèche de la cathédrale, c'est bien cela. Mais justement tu peux le montrer dès le moment où tu as "traité" la philosophie, c'est-à-dire non pas en lui ôtant sa dynamique ou son importance, mais la prétention qu'elle serait supérieure ou qu'elle survolerait les autres disciplines. Elle ne survole pas l'art de l'architecte. Et pourtant, elle est dans la flèche.

Schmid: Pourquoi ce terme de "réminiscience"?

Laruelle: J'appelle Réminiscience, un mot synthétique composé artificiellement, en parodie de la réminiscence platonicienne, qui est l'acte de mémoire se rapportant au savoir, savoir que l'on est sensé avoir acquis, mais en tant qu'êtres humains, on a plus ou moins oublié, et qui revient, qui est objet d'un souvenir. Alors j'appelle réminiscience la combinaison de la mémoire philosophique et de la science, la science elle-même partagée d'ailleurs en générique et en quantique. La science la plus fondamentale pour moi c'est d'une certaine manière la mécanique quantique qui remplace la physique newtonienne ou physique kantienne. Cela se passe à l'intérieur de cette triplicité où il y a un axe fondamental, qui tient debout l'ensemble, et qui est lui-même tenu debout par les deux contreforts que sont le générique et le quantique qui la jouxtent.

Schmid: La quantique a eu une importance là-dedans? Par rapport à la mécanique classique. La mécanique classique, c'est des textes avec une alternance d'équations et de langage naturel. C'est l'illusion que l'on parle des objets macroscopiques. C'est l'illusion que nous sommes dans un espace euclidien à trois dimensions. La quantique, qu'est-ce qu'elle fait? Elle ne parle plus d'objets. Elle parle d'états, elle parle d'opérateurs, elle parle d'équations, elle parle de mathématiques, elle distingue assez soigneusement les mathématiques et l'interprétation. Ce n'est que des mathématiques, et d'autre part les physiciens doivent avoir chaque fois une interprétation. On voit des physiciens quantiques faire des livres qui expliquent la quantique, c'est très important, parce que cette explication doit être inventée, ce qui n'est pas le cas pour la mécanique classique. Et justement, cette caractéristique de la quantique qui ne s'occupe plus d'objets au sens macroscopique permet de faire passer la philosophie à un autre niveau où elle ne porte plus sur les objets, etc., où son dynamisme porte plutôt sur les flux, sur des nombres, des flux, des couleurs, des charmes, etc. Quelque chose qui nous échappe un peu, mais nous permet d'aborder la philosophie avec d'autres choses comme de la musique ou l'art dont nous ne pouvons pas parler autrement. La quantique a ouvert les champs. Mais au travers de mon travail de terrain, je vois surtout des multiplicités de la biologie et de sa gamme de disciplines. C'est aussi une instance, mais qui n'est pas encore la dernière, elle permet d'ajouter des axiomes intermédiaires entre l'Un et ce que j'appelle la "multiplicité de droit" des philosophies.

Prof. Dr. François Laruelle, Université Paris Nanterre,
Collège International de Philosophie, francois.laruelle[at]free.fr
Prof. Dr. Anne-Françoise Schmid, MINES ParisTech,
annefschmid[at]gmail.com

Références

Careri, Giovanni. *La torpeur des Ancêtres. Juifs et chrétiens dans la chapelle Sixtine*. Paris: EHESS, 2013.
Laruelle, François. *Phénomène et Différence. Essai sur Ravaisson*. Paris, Klincksieck, 1971.
Laruelle, François. *En dernière humanité. La nouvelle science écologique*. Paris: Cerf, 2015.

HARMONIZING VOICES:
FRANÇOIS LARUELLE AND ANTHONY PAUL SMITH

An Interview with Anthony Paul Smith (Philadelphia)
by Mark William Westmoreland (Villanova)

Abstract

The following interview of Mark William Westmoreland with Anthony Paul Smith – well-known scholar and translator of François Laruelle – considers both implications and extensions of Laruelle's non-philosophy for contemporary thought. Smith has helped bring about a surge of interest in Laruelle due to his many translations of his texts as well as being the author or co-editor of several books on Laruelle. Discussed are in particular the difficulties and joys of translating and the usefulness of Laruelle's thought for Smith's own work, especially in environmental and animal studies. Also considered are some themes of non-philosophy, the adaptability of Laruelle's thought for various disciplines, as well as new paths for Laruelle studies – new, unforeseen landscapes and uses of non-philosophy – that explore social phenomena such as race, racism, sexism, victim a.o.

Keywords: Laruelle, translation, continental philosophy, race, ecology

Westermoreland: Thank you, Anthony, for according me this interview about François Laruelle and your own work. How did you come across Laruelle? Did you encounter his work while you were a student at DePaul or Nottingham?

Smith: I first came across Laruelle's ideas in John Ó Maoilearca's *Post-Continental Philosophy: An Outline* shortly after it first published by Continuum back in 2007. So, this was during my time as a student at the University of Nottingham when I was especially interested in the four thinkers of immanence that his book examines (Gilles Deleuze, Alain Badiou, Michel Henry, and of course François Laruelle). John was publishing under his Anglicized surname Mullarkey at the time, and I had found his work on Bergson incredibly rich and helpful for my own research (my MA examined philosophical resources in Bergson and Deleuze/Guattari for rethinking the practice of ecological restoration). In the UK, or at least at Nottingham, students are not expected to buy books for their coursework like they are in the US. The campus bookstore would just stock relatively random things, and I came across John's book there and bought it.

Westermoreland: You went to Nottingham to study alongside philosopher Philip Goodchild, correct? What drew you to Goodchild's work?

Smith: Right, I went to Nottingham to work with the Philip, whose 2002 *Capitalism and Religion: The Price of Piety* had changed my whole understanding of the world and philosophy. It was his work that had directed me to Deleuze and Guattari and that radical line of thinking in France and Italy centered around thinking immanence and univocity. But Nottingham was also home to a particularly pugnacious school of philosophico-theological thought known as Radical Orthodoxy which held that Deleuze was a particularly pungent example of a kind of philosophical error in turning away from transcendence that led to what they termed "nihilism." By this term they meant the decline of the West and in particular Christianity, and so astute readers and those already familiar with this school of thinking can see certain markers of white supremacist thought, specifically in a kind of highbrow European and Christian modality. Anyhow, dealing with this school of thought was in some ways really stultifying, but I have to give them credit for accurately seeing the link between ontology and politics, between being and ethics. They happen to be wrong about pretty much everything else, but there was a certain seriousness and concreteness with which philosophy and theology had to be studied in that environment that I took seriously.

Westermoreland: What was it about Ó Maoilearca's book thought caught your attention?

Smith: John's own critique of Deleuze in *Post-Continental Philosophy* helped me to gain some purchase on what I found dissatisfying in Deleuze's treatment of immanence, while avoiding the nostalgic draw of orthodox Christian accounts of transcendence. I think that John's critique of Deleuze was partly something he come to in his own thinking and partly through the critique of Deleuze found in Laruelle's work which in turn also dovetailed with Philip's critique. Essentially, for these three thinkers, Deleuze's understanding of immanence transposed the thought of immanence into a transcendence. This meant that

Deleuze's philosophy was a philosophy *of* immanence, rather than a philosophy *in* or *through* immanence – an immanence-philosophy.

That really intrigued me and John's suggestion in *Post-Continental Philosophy* that both Henry's and Laruelle's philosophies offered resources to rethink immanence in an immanent way lead me to file his name in the back of my head. At the time I was an MA student and so did not have a lot of disposable income and our university library didn't have any books by Laruelle. I tried to make sense of the few incredibly difficult and contextless articles that had been translated into English, but could not really work them out at the time. My interest was piqued again when a number of us in the Philosophical Theology track at Nottingham read Ray Brassier's 2007 *Nihil Unbound: Enlightenment and Extinction*. While John's reading opened up a certain possibility for thinking through Laruelle's non-philosophy, Brassier's work was all about elimination and cutting away. Something about this difference rooted in the same reading, a possibility that John had already accounted for in *Post-Continental Philosophy*, really intrigued me as well.

Finally I got a few of Laruelle's books and I started reading them. But it wasn't the technical aspect of immanence that first grabbed me in his thought. The first book of his I read cover to cover was *Le Christ futur. Une leçon d'hérésie*. I had escaped to Paris from Nottingham for a few days and bought a used copy in Gibert Jeune. Here I found a Laruelle concerned not just with technical philosophical questions around immanence, but with suffering, with a certain gnostic hatred of the World, with an unflinching analysis of philosophy's role in constructing that world and obscuring or denying suffering, and I was moved by it all. I became somewhat obsessed with the terminology, with the syntax, and with the way of thinking. I saw in that book the performance of philosophy *in* immanence.

Westermoreland: You've devoted a lot of energy to working on Laruelle. What are your scholarly plans for the next year with regard to Laruelle or otherwise? Five years from now, what do you imagine yourself to be doing?

Smith: I have found Laruelle's work really helpful, but I also saw in his work a kind of escape from the way that Continental philosophy has been done in the US where we write monographs about what this French or that German philosopher's work says. I don't mean to minimize that work and I am really thankful for the strong training I received in the history of European philosophy at DePaul as an undergraduate. But it just is not what I want to do with my life. I think those of us working with Laruelle's ideas and body of work have done a relatively good job of avoiding setting up a journal of Laruelle Studies or the like. Laruelle has worked a lot of this out, he's discovered a certain kind of thinking, but what has always interested me, and I think what interests him, is the way that practice can be used in a variety of contexts without each page being exegesis of his books or the minutia of his archive.

So, after publishing two secondary sources on Laruelle in 2016, I want to get back to work that I think is non-philosophical but is not worried about personal fidelity to the individual François Laruelle and his interests at the level of application. As François joked in an interview that John, Marjorie Gracieuse, and I conducted with him in 2010, "Laruelle does not exist." While I am glad to know François and his incredible kindness, along with that of his partner and fellow philosopher Anne-Françoise Schmid, I think part of that kindness and part of his ethics is to refuse being a kind of "Name of the Father" that authorizes this or that orthodoxy.

In terms of my own work, I tend to think in terms of philosophical engagement with religious materials (both theological and lived) and environmental theory. So, I have two major projects that I have been working on in these two areas though I see them as interlinked. First, I want to follow-up my work in environmental philosophy with a second book that examines questions of colonialism and race in ecological thought. By ecological thought I both mean scientific thinking and what sometimes goes under the name environmental humanities or political ecology. A friend and incredible thinker named Amaryah Armstrong, who is currently finishing a PhD at Vanderbilt, read my *A Non-Philosophical Theory of Nature: Ecologies of Thought* (I'll never forgive the publisher for bizarrely reversing the title and subtitle) and encouraged me to engage with work being done in Black Studies around similar questions of heretical thinking, identity, the perversity of the natural, and a rejection of simplistic naturalistic thinking (which I think has nothing to do with the actual study of nature). I think that the environmental humanities trades on a reputation of radicality simply because of how distressing and catastrophic the problem of climate change is. We have all of these white scholars – and I'm one of them, and I know I don't get cookies for pointing out that my colleagues are also white – who are talking about living in the end times and rethinking the poststructuralist death of "man" without any serious engagement with ontological questions and without engaging with the important work of Katherine McKittrick, Hortense Spillers, Frank B. Wilderson, Saidiya Hartman, Jared Sexton, and others. This work is devastating to the new orthodoxies and the pretense to radicality found in the vast majority of the environmental humanities. I've laid out this charge in a long review essay of some recent books in the environmental humanities[1] and I am using that criticism as a starting point for an unflinching analysis of ecological thought's anti-Blackness.

The other project is an examination of theodicy as philosophical form. Again, this comes out of studying both Laruelle's work and the various projects sometimes collected under the name of Afro-pessimism. It's really important to point out that none of these thinkers are the same, they have different projects and the ways in which academia brands people or tries to stir up conflicts is even more problematic when it comes to Black scholars and how they are treated by a white supremacist academy. I am trying to work with their work as materials but with an awareness of how white scholars often appropriate and re-brand more radical work. I have no illusions that I'll ever reach the stature of these scholars and really what I am trying to do is take seriously the universal reach of Black studies that respects that the work of Black scholars is not simply a disinterested academic enterprise, as Christina Sharpe very passionately and powerfully argues in her recent *In the Wake*. So, I am using a kind of conjugation of this new philosophical work in Black studies with Laruelle's work to turn on the history of white European philosophy and show the ways it justifies this World and engages in various theodical forms of thinking. I've published a few historical essays on Bergson and Simone Weil that are the first fruits of this work, but the book will be less historical in scope and focused more on the form itself. I think that both Black studies and Laruelle have this core rejection of theodicy, of any justification for the world as it is, that unites them as a Gnostic form of thought which can cut through so much of the weakness and timidity of philosophical thinking today. They, and the work being undertaken by these scholars in Black studies more so than even Laruelle, gets at this connection between ontology and politics, between Being and ethics, that matters and touches on the reality of suffering in the world – of suffering the world itself.

Westermoreland: You have written that philosophy is in the midst of an identity crisis. While this is a very old concern for philosophers, might it be something we need to consider again? Has philosophy come to its end, with its questions shattered into the hands of a thousand disciplines? I certainly hope not. Perhaps it's a question of what should be done with philosophy rather than us being finished with it.

---

[1] Online available at https://itself.blog/2017/07/06/on-the-use-and-abuse-of-objects-for-the-environmental-humanities-recent-books-in-object-oriented-ontology-and-ecotheory/

Smith: We have to distinguish between the practice of thought, which can take the name philosophy, and the academic discipline siloed off with discrete problems, brands, ways bright graduate students have to sell themselves on an oversaturated market, tenure requirements, textbooks, and all the other accoutrements of intellectual life under capitalism. I think that for those who are invested in being recognizable to the contemporary academic job market as philosophers, then yes, there is a real identity crisis going on. And I don't mean to be pat at all. There are good reasons for being so invested. It's quite literally a matter of survival for many people and there are certain practices of rigor and the like that having some kind of disciplinary boundaries can engender. But I think philosophy in this catachrestic sense is about something more abiding than I hope capitalism and its abuse of our lives ends up being. For Laruelle, philosophy is not ending. It's something that manifests out of human practice. He does seek to limit or disempower the sufficiency and arrogance of philosophy, but that's not the same thing as calling for its end.

I think in his more recent work Laruelle has backed away from the more trenchant calls for philosophy's disempowerment that people took as heralding its end. For me, though, I really do think we should look for philosophical work outside of the bounds of disciplinary philosophy. That's not surprising though since my material wellbeing is not predicated on recognition as a philosopher. I'm employed as a professor in a Religion & Theology Department and while I'm not really recognizable there either, as a discipline the study of religion has more diversity and possibility for survival in smaller niches than professional philosophers do. Still, that "luck" or whatever we might call it does allow me to see the way philosophical work takes place in scientific ecology, in politico-religious communities and their traditions of thinking, and in other less academically respectable places. That doesn't mean that philosophy has shattered into a thousand disciplines in the way some declension narratives have it, but that philosophy in the catachrestic sense is always already fractal and perverse in nature.

Westermoreland: His work tends to engage with the transcendental structures of philosophical thinking. How would you position Laruelle among his contemporaries with regard to the use of philosophy? Or, put differently, to what extent is he outside the canon?

Smith: Laruelle is very much a part of the tradition, though probably not fated to be a part of the canon. He is concerned with creating a science of philosophy and then making use of philosophy. In that way he's not so different from other French philosophers of his generation. Deleuze, Derrida, and Irigaray, to pick just three important examples, thought through the history of philosophy or through the philosophical texts of others. What makes Laruelle different is his stance towards this use of philosophy. Deleuze and Derrida, though perhaps not Irigaray, are concerned with extending philosophy, with reproducing philosophy, and Laruelle is concerned with its disempowerment or "degrowth" (one translation of *dépotentialisation* that has nice ecological connections). It's an important distinction, one that links Laruelle with more radical strands of thought.

Westermoreland: Are there aspects of Laruelle's thought that you take to be significant but haven't made their way into the secondary literature? For example, at the heart of Laruelle's work is the idea that the ordinary and generic human is something to be defended. Things like technology and politics are forms of authority that seek in some way to harass and murder the human, but which may also be disempowered by the human and used in more therapeutic modes.

Smith: Agreed. I don't think we have really worked through what his work has to add to discussions of technology and politics in relation to our existence as human beings. In some ways his work on the identity of the human is more similar to Sylvia Wynter's project than it is to his contemporaries like Foucault. Both Laruelle's and Wynter's work shows us how the construction of the false universal of Man is predicated upon a certain kind of philosophical sufficiency and where Wynter shows us the history of that project, Laruelle traces the transcendental structures of it. I think examining these transcendental structures are very important and can add to these discussions.

Westermoreland: In *Ecologies of Thought*, you employed Laruelle's non-philosophy for thinking about ecology. This text might be seen, among other things, as a useful addition to environmental studies. Are there particular fields of study that you think would benefit from Laruelle's work?

Smith: Laruelle's work doesn't lend itself to imposition. I'm been pleasantly surprised by the ways he gets taken up in performance studies, visual art, and most recently in the study of Buddhism. I'd like to continue to be surprised. What Laruelle has done with his non-philosophy is create something that people can put to use in their fields, but how that ends up looking really depends on their performance of the thought.

Westermoreland: Earlier you mentioned that you plan on writing more about questions of colonialism and race in ecological thought. The two of us have collaborated before on panels focused on colonialism, racism, and ecology, and I'm excited to see what you'll publish on this. With regard to Laruelle, do you think his work offers us anything useful for when we consider the ills of racism, sexism, homophobia, xenophobia, etc.? I'm thinking here of the French philosophical tradition of the 20th and 21st centuries with regard to race in particular. For instance, there is only one place in Ricoeur's oeuvre where race appears – in an interview where Ricoeur is asked about the educational system in the United States. Balibar, however, regularly writes about race and neo-racism. Recently, Magali Bessone has published a book, *Sans distinction de race?*, which offers a genealogy of the concept of race, a topic that has caught on much more in the United States than in France. In short, with few exceptions, contemporary French philosophy doesn't seem that interested in questions about race and racism.

Smith: Yes, I think he does. Laruelle's work isn't really practical in the usual sense of that word and so what he offers isn't on the level of important works in anti-racist or anti-sexist organizing. As with all of his work he focuses at the level of the transcendental structures of our philosophical thinking. So, the ways that his work will be useful to analyzing anti-black racism or other forms of discrimination are not going to be explicit or obvious in the way that Balibar's have been, but when recognized they also won't seem added on like some of his contemporaries. What Laruelle shows is that central to philosophical thinking, to its very identity as philosophy, is a decision that operates by dividing up – or more violently, that cuts up – whatever it claims to attempt to know. This division of whatever object of knowledge is then unified by philosophy under some third term. Now this might seem to be a particularly novel claim, since many philosophers after Nietzsche (if not before) have criticized philosophy for this kind of approach. What makes Laruelle important is the acidity of his critique. He shows us that this decision is at work in philosophies who work out of a position of transcendence, like Platonism, but also transcendental philosophies, like Kant, and, more dangerously, philosophies of immanence, like Deleuze. I say acidity, because Laruelle's general critique of philosophy does not allow for us to find any refuge from the criticism. There is no "good version" of philosophy (a phrase I'm using from my friend Daniel Colucciello Barber) that is left untouched by his universal acid. It's a through-going critique of philosophy from within the male white European tradition that can be useful to rethinking the very practices of thought and refuses to constantly seek philosophy's innocence. It links up to certain projects, like that of the early Orlando Patterson, who showed how our conception of freedom is tied conceptually and politically to slavery. There is no conception of freedom without an absolute point of unfreedom. Laruelle tries to move beyond this kind of thinking through what he calls unilateral duality, he seeks to retool the machinery of philosophy to think in a stranger way, like showing how freedom is grounded in unfreedom and what it might look like to think from the radical immanence of that unfreedom instead.

But it is important to note that, while I think Laruelle's work is unique in this way and is useful for these sorts of projects, it doesn't mean I think he is free from error or that others couldn't or wouldn't use his work in anti-black or misogynistic ways. I could very easily see other thinkers turning to Laruelle as a renewed version of the universal image of the human that somehow "doesn't see race," whereas I see Laruelle's ethical work as being more radically tied to seeing the generic manifestation of the human in those subject positions that have historically and transcendentally been excluded or exiled from the universal. I've tried to lay this out more rigorously and thoroughly in *Laruelle: A Stranger Thought*. While in my short guidebook to *Principles of Non-Philosophy* I located Laruelle within the various European philosophical traditions he engages with, in *Laruelle: A Stranger Thought* I found it more interesting and fecund to show how Laruelle's work may linkup with more radical forms of thought that are generally excluded from the bounds of disciplinary philosophy.

Westermoreland: Can you explain Laruelle's concept of the victim? The victim is Laruelle's preferred example of the subject position that is, at worst excluded from or, at best, pitied by the philosophers. He lays this out most explicitly in a book-length interview translated as *Intellectuals and Power* and in the recent *General Theory of Victims*. In each case the victim is not someone to pity, the victim is not described as lacking agency, none of that. It's not really a theory of the subject position of the victim; that would be an example of the very thing that Laruelle is criticizing throughout his work where philosophy *speaks about* the victim rather than *thinks according to* the victim.

Smith: He says in *General Theory of Victims* that his goal is to move from the image of the victim to the concept. In that way thinking according to the victim allows Laruelle to investigate the way that world is formed philosophically. Earlier I said that Laruelle's analysis of philosophy reveals a fundamental violence that is about cutting up objects so that they, in the end, come to reflect philosophy's structures itself rather than their fundamentally immanent realness. His "victimology" is another example of that. So instead of thinking the victim from a position of pity, Laruelle is able to see that the way the harassment and murder of human beings, which constitutes their victimhood, also constitutes the world itself. What is it that creates a hallucination of a human being into a victim but the very need to craft a world, to create a unity of experience, to create a narrative that grounds the psychic coherence of those who persecute against those who are persecuted. Power is exactly one of the terms that Laruelle identifies as a philosophical transcendental that is used to unite terms that are separated, like victim and persecutor or victim and oppressor or even victim and criminal (which is the most reversible of relations under the so-called criminal justice system). I think there are really important works that look at that third term differently than Laruelle does, but what Laruelle aims to do is actually think the victim outside of that framework of power. Again, we can see ways in which his work is doing similar things in a different register to very powerful and radical work elsewhere. So instead of thinking how to gain power, an obsession of the disempowered Left for example, he wants to think how power might be the very term that needs to be broken with and how breaking the relation of victim and oppressor can show other modalities of subjectivity or survival within the world.

I could say quite a bit more here about how Laruelle is drawing on the gnostic ultra-Maoism of the early work of Christian Jambet and Guy Lardreau, but the victim is generally a very gnostic notion in his work. The world is not something to be saved for Laruelle, only the human is. But human beings are also the very demiurge that has created that world. This is the point where I start to have some differences from Laruelle in the thinking of the victim. As with most of his work he seeks the most abstract and generic point possible. I don't think we can quite do that with victims in an easy way or at least in a way that avoids a kind of implicit liberal philosophy that obscures the further reality of the victim.

Westermoreland: We are always already conditioned by our socio-historical context, and this context, at our current conjuncture, is one marked by the ills of racism. There is a racial asymmetry that colorblindness ("doesn't see race") ignores and, consequently, perpetuates. Recall Fanon in *Black Skin, White Masks*, "All round me the white man […] all this whiteness that burns me." This is sadly a white normative world.

Smith: There is a question, at the global level, of who this human demiurge that creates the world. Which particular subjects benefit from the creation of this failed world, which despite being, as Laruelle calls it, a hallucination, still has the objective power of death for some humans cast into these oppressed subject positions? I think it is quite clear that it has been the creation of a white world (a phrase in Fanon's *Black Skin, White Masks* that I am drawn to) and it benefits those subjects most who are further away from the most extreme and excluded subject positions, like the Slave and Indigenous, or the less extreme like the Foreigner. When Laruelle calls the philosopher to a position of "compassion" instead of pity in *General Theory of Victims*, he means a co-suffering and ultimately I think that can only look like becoming nothing in the eyes of the world.

Westermoreland: Both of the previous concerns also relate to the notion of strangers? Is there overlap in Laruelle's thinking about victims and strangers? How does the notion of stranger differ from Derrida's other or Kant's abstract universalizing of every person as an end in themselves?

Smith: There is an overlap and it's again at the level of what I have been calling the subject position of the human or the hallucination of a worldly self. The Stranger is found throughout Laruelle's earlier work and it's structurally very similar to the victim in those works. I personally like this move because it's actually a response in his thinking to what some have called the obsession with the Other in poststructuralist philosophy. As a philosophical concept the Stranger is far less obfuscatory regarding power or other means of oppression than the Other. I'm thinking here of Levinas' failure to see in the Palestinians the face of the Other in the interview where he is asked about the 1982 massacres at the Palestinian refugee camps of Sabra and Shatila or of the way in which Derrida's formulation of *tout autre est tout autre* can again obscure what I called the human demiurge who creates the world. The Stranger usually translates *l'Étranger* in Laruelle's work, but in French it also means the foreigner or alien. It's clear that Laruelle intends these meanings in his use and this gives his thinking a more concrete ethical and political character than Levinas' apolitical ethical Other does. In his work on the *l'Étranger* Laruelle is saying that this is the position of the foreigner that has to define any politics and any ethics, not the citizen. Again, it isn't a matter of universalizing in the sense of subtracting qualities away to get to the essence of the human, but of starting from the absolute point of deracination to think that essence. To do that one cannot simply think from some point of philosophical universalization, but one must think from a subject position even if the point is the abolition of subjects or selves in the name of the real human.

Westermoreland: Can you shed some light on the joys and difficulties of translating Laruelle's works into English?

Smith: Translators have a really difficult job. It's impossible, really, in the best of situations. With a thinker like Laruelle there are two main difficulties. First, there is his French itself and, second, there is the way he uses terminology and ideas from across the history of philosophy without always tipping his reader off to the source or tradition he's referencing.

So, let's talk about his French first. Alex Dubilet, another translator of Laruelle's work, once told me that Laruelle read to him like a French philosopher who OD'd on German and I think that is right. French lends itself to very complex sentences generally, but Laruelle takes it up a notch in most of his books. As a translator you have a choice here and, in my view, neither of the two options are particularly great. First, you can do what Scott Davidson does in his translations of Michel Henry (who also has this Germanic style to his phenomenological writing) and either break up these French sentences into English so that they are more readable or you can leave them in their current state and risk confusion. I think Davidson's translations are great and he has good reasons for his choice, but there is also something about Laruelle's expression being an expression of radical immanence that has always made me and usually my co-translators stick to his structure. It can be a maddening experience to try and follow the grammar at times, but native French speakers report similar experiences and so if translation is about translating the experience of reading across languages then I think we're doing on ok job there. I have also tended towards more literal translations, which I think might be somewhat of a prejudice from my work in Medieval philosophy and theology where literal translations of Aquinas, Scotus, and others were more common. I think, for Laruelle, the untranslatability of a number of his jokes and cleverness gives way to privileging the ideas. I really hate missing those and try my best to find a good translation that captures them, but often they just have to be explained in a footnote and as we all know there's nothing funnier than having a joke explained to you.

Secondly, as I said, there is his use of the history of philosophy without referencing. Therefore, anyone translating Laruelle has to be well versed in the history of European philosophy, from the Ancient Greeks to 19th and 20th century German philosophy, and contemporary French philosophy as well as a smattering of work done in psychoanalysis, quantum physics, Western and Eastern Christianity, and various Gnostic philosophies and theologies. I'm very lucky to have received such a strong background in the history of philosophy as an undergraduate and so matching those terminology choices with standard translations or deciding to translate them a different way is weirdly enjoyable for me. I hope it makes reading Laruelle and situating his ideas within a certain constellation of ideas easier as well.

Westermoreland: Thank you again for engaging in this conversation. Do you have any final thoughts about translating?

Smith: To be honest, I find translation to be mostly heartbreaking. Either by yourself or with someone else you get to work on this massive project, devote hundreds and hundreds of hours to working through the text, move through various drafts, send it to other readers, try to incorporate their remarks or get lost on trails that go nowhere, work with copy editors of various skill levels, stare directly in the face of your own inadequacies and idiocies, work to improve over and over again, and at the end of all that hard work the best you can hope for is that it isn't a complete failure and that, if it gets read, the graduate students looking to fill up seminar time don't spend all their time nitpicking the translation choices or pointing out the errors that invariably will exist. The joys that come are intellectual in nature. Through translating I take the text on more fully than I do simply reading it. I think through it in a new way, I am writing the text myself. It isn't matter of becoming a conduit for the divine word – I'm suspicious that this is even possible – but there's a certain harmonizing of Laruelle's voice and my own. There's something joyful in that.

Dr. Anthony Paul Smith, Department of Religion,
La Salle University, smithanthony[at]lasalle.edu
Dr. Mark William Westmoreland, Department of Philosophy,
Villanova University, mark.westmoreland[at]villanova.edu

NON-PHILOSOPHY, SOCIAL ACTION, AND PERFORMANCE

CONSTANCE L. MUI (New Orleans)
JULIEN S. MURPHY (Portland, Maine)

Victims, Power and Intellectuals: Laruelle and Sartre

Abstract

In two recent works, Intellectuals and Power and General Theory of Victims, François Laruelle offers a critique of the public intellectual, including Jean-Paul Sartre, claiming such intellectuals have a disregard for victims of crimes against humanity. Laruelle insists that the victim has been left out of philosophy and displaced by an abstract pursuit of justice. He offers a non- philosophical approach that reverses the victim/intellectual dyad and calls for compassionate insurrection. In this paper, we probe Laruelle's critique of the committed intellectual's obligations to victims, specifically, through an examination of Sartre's "A Plea for Intellectuals." We hope to show the value of Laruelle's theory on victims, crime and power for imagining future-oriented intellectuals.

Keywords: Laruelle, Sartre, power, intellectuals, victim, non-philosophy, compassion

In *Intellectuals and Power*, an interview with Philippe Petit that was translated into English shortly after the Boston Marathon bombing in 2013, François Laruelle offers a critique of public intellectuals. He faults French intellectuals such as Jean-Paul Sartre for their disregard for victims of crimes against humanity, and their willingness in some instances to legitimate atrocities. Laruelle is equally dissatisfied with philosophy itself, contending that in its pursuit of abstract justice, philosophy has all but forgotten the actual victims of injustice. As a result, philosophy has failed to recognize an exclusive human identity for victims. Laruelle insists that victims are central to humanity, and we must rethink our obligations toward them by revising our notion of the intellectual who speaks in their behalf. With this in mind, he offers a post-continental approach to understanding the relationship between intellectuals and victims in his recent book, *General Theory of Victims*. Our purpose is to assess the value of Laruelle's critique of intellectuals in the two works through a Laruellean reading of Sartre's later view of engaged intellectuals in "A Plea for Intellectuals." (Sartre 1976) Our analysis seeks to show the value of Laruelle's work for charting a path forward for intellectuals in the current century.

Recent massacres in the U.S. jettison a focus on victims in public discourse. Mass casualties by gun violence in America are etched in the public consciousness and referenced by location: Sutherland Springs, Texas (2017); Las Vegas (2017); Dallas (2016); Orlando (2016); San Bernardino (2015); Charleston (2015); Sandy Hook (2012); Aurora (2012); and Tucson (2011). Sadly, this is by no means an exhaustive list, as attacks on innocent bystanders by fellow citizens are becoming increasingly common.[1] Assailants who often act alone use assault weapons to maximize casualties at a scale that is unfathomable. Despite the odds, just about anyone can imagine being the next victim. In fact, concurrent with this writing is the Las Vegas shootings, in which a gunman fired 280 rounds into an outdoor music concert crowd of thousands on the Vegas Strip, killing 58 people and injuring 546 others, all within ten minutes. (Belson, 2017) Elsewhere in the war-torn part of the Sinai Peninsula, there are 305 dead from a single attack on a Sufi mosque. (Walsh and Youssef, 2017) What we mark here is the new reality of civil society, where massacres of war zones have been transported through lone assailants to our churches, schools, and public arenas in America.

Victims of gun violence in a heavily-armed technological society typically receive considerable media attention, even though none has resulted in appreciable political change. What have remained largely invisible to the public eye are victims of a different kind of violence, namely, economic deprivation. We rarely pay attention to the homeless death rate, even though in the past year alone, there were 210 homeless people who died on the streets in Los Angeles, (Luppi, 2017) 117 in Utah, (Anderson, 2017) 118 in Nashville, (Koehn, 2017) and 37 in the small city of Portland, Maine. (Hoey, 2017) The body count from other cities across the country is buried deeply in media coverage, if covered at all. Likewise, there are no official statistics on impoverished victims who die from lack of medical attention, from malnutrition, or from fires related to substandard housing.

---

[1] These episodes of mass shootings are not exclusively an American phenomenon. To cite one example, in 2012 a lone shooter in Norway also deployed a small bomb to kill more than seventy young people at a summer camp.

Victims of all stripes and the increasing role of public intellectuals who would speak in their defense are important issues worthy of philosophical examination. Laruelle rejects the treatment of victims as negligible collateral damage, posing the question in the preface of *General Theory of Victims*, "If the executioner is the cornerstone of society (Joseph de Maistre), why would the victim not be the cornerstone of humanity?" (2015b, ii) In view of the rising incidents of victims of violence, and of the fact that it has been over fifty years since Sartre theorized about the engaged intellectual, it is time to rethink the relationship between victims and intellectuals. Laruelle offers a new approach for framing that relationship, one that focuses on a theory of victims that places the victim in a generic, undetermined humanity, and the important role of intellectuals in making a case for their humanity. What sort of intellectual is needed now?

It is important to note that both *Intellectuals and Power* and *General Theory of Victims* are written as works of "non-philosophy". They challenge the idea of the public intellectual by calling out philosophy's authority. Laruelle, who does not regard himself as an intellectual in the traditional sense, goes beyond the trajectory of Sartre, Foucault, and Deleuze to develop a new conception of victims and, in that connection, a new understanding of the intellectual/victim relationship. The subtitle of *Intellectuals and Power*, "*The Insurrection of the Victim*" signals this move. It is the victim, he claims, that exposes the limits of power that undergirds the very position of the public intellectual. Through a non-philosophical analysis, Laruelle presents a new victim/intellectual dyad that forms the crux of his general theory. In this analysis Laurelle also offers a sketch of the intellectual for the future.

We begin with a description of Laruelle's non-philosophy to show the theoretical difference in the zone of operation between philosophy and non-philosophy. We then draw comparisons between Laruelle's and Sartre's accounts of the proper roles of intellectuals. This is followed by an examination of Laruelle's theory of victims, which is based what such concepts as 'Victim-in-person' and 'Human-in-person.' We trace how Laruelle applies this theory to reframe the victim/intellectual dyad. We conclude with an assessment of the degree to which Sartre's committed intellectual aligns with Laruelle's generic intellectual, as well as some observations concerning the future of the post-Sartrean intellectual for post-continental (non) philosophy.

Laruelle's Non-Philosophy

Any assessment of Laruelle's critique of intellectuals must be understood within his non-philosophy, a term he uses to refer to a rethinking of philosophy. It could easily be assumed that non-philosophy, like Sartre's works of fiction, has nothing to do with theory or reason or the logical representation of thought. This would be mistaken, as Laruelle's non-philosophy is a theory-wielding discourse that looks quite a bit like philosophy. As such, non-philosophy is not a refutation of philosophy or a meta-philosophy, but an inquiry that requires the use of philosophy, much like non-Euclidean geometry can only be understood by its relationship to Euclidean geometry. It is not anti-philosophical but is critical of philosophy in a positive or corrective way; it digests and transforms the very content of philosophy. Precisely as non-philosophy, Laruelle says, it has the advantage of avoiding some of philosophy's major problems. A central problem Laurelle identifies involves the long tradition in philosophy of assessing reality first by reducing it to dualistic or dialectical oppositions, such as that between immanence and transcendence, or between being and existence. From this oppositional starting point, philosophers are able to secure and legitimate their position as grand unifiers of a diffuse complex of opposing structures. Rejecting the traditional enterprise as illusory at best, Laruelle claims that non-philosophy begins with reality as a basic, undivided, undetermined unity. This alternative starting point offers a new way of examining humanity in direct relation to the One, prior to difference. As one critic put it, Laruelle seeks to "engage reality from the position of the immanence of reality itself." (Burk 2012, xiii) The aim of his non-philosophical approach is to build a theory of humanity alongside philosophy.

The term non-philosophy can be traced in the continental tradition to a lecture by Merleau-Ponty, entitled, "Philosophy and Non-Philosophy Since Hegel." Laruelle adopted the term in his rethinking of the Real, which he characterizes as "the One", or "radical immanence". These are two key concepts in Laurelle that were missing in his study of Deleuze, Levinas and Derrida, but discovered in the work of Michel Henry. (Mullarkey and Smith 2012, 239) A notion of radical immanence, one that included the possibility of transcendence, can be found in Henry's phenomenology. (Henry 2008) However, in Laruelle's understanding of the term, the One displaces not only Heideggerian Being, but also Henry's concept of transcendence. It describes the human Real without identifying any ontological difference between, say, Being and existence, or immanence and transcendence. And yet the Real is not to be confused with essence. Rather, it is the basis of lived reality (similar to Henry's notion of "life"). It is all that exists—autonomous, non-relational, non-representable, undefinable, and unknowable. In a similar vein, Laruelle provides an intrepid defense of immanence, one that eludes philosophy, phenomenology, psychoanalysis, and the human sciences. He likens immanence to interiority, in the sense that it cannot reveal itself from outside of itself. Further, Laruelle says that if it exists, it is no longer real. (Laruelle, 2013, 37) But as Ray Brassier notes, the Real is not nothing, it is not "Sartre's nihilating 'for-itself' puncturing the opacity of the 'in-itself.'" (Brassier 2007, 137) Laruelle's refusal to define the human has been likened to Sartre's rejection of any definable human essence, although, as John O'Maoilearca notes, Laruelle goes beyond this by rejecting nothingness as well, in so far as it is understood in relation to Being. (O'Maoilearca 2015, 183)

Laruelle challenges us to engage in non-philosophy to examine humanity at a level of abstraction beyond the relationship between being and nothingness, to understand humanity generically as indivisible. Laruelle says repeatedly that non-philosophy is the practice of thinking according to the Real—that is, thinking the irreducible that is presupposed in thought, separated from the world. Non-philosophy is that which determines "in-the-last-instance a subject *for* the relation of representation and the unrepresentable proper to philosophy" (Laurelle 2015a, 32). As such, it is the radical inversion of philosophy (ibid., 48). Philosophy labors under the old categories that prevent it from being a liberatory tool. Laruelle believes that while we are "condemned to philosophy" and to history, and "condemned to confront the global crime-form" (ibid., 126), non-philosophy can best assist us both in theorizing without totalization, and in foregrounding victims of mass crimes against humanity.

The difficulty in comprehending Laruelle's non-philosophy is that, although it takes the content of philosophy for its content, it resists being understood within philosophy. But if philosophy cannot be used to understand non-philosophy, then the whole enterprise of non-philosophy is thwarted from the outset. Brassier, for instance, argues that "to claim I harbor some sort of preontological understanding of my own being-human is to plunge straight back into Heidegger's *Dasein*. Alternatively, to assert, as Laruelle does, that one already 'knows' oneself to be human in and through radical immanence, is simply to misuse the verb, 'to know'". (Brassier 2007, 137) Brassier is right, Laruelle's intent is preontological (it is easy to see Henry's influence here). It is no surprise he has garnered criticism for being overly obtuse, even though *Victims* is credited with being his most accessible work. Others, such as John Mullarkey, wonder about the extent to which Laruelle's non-philosophy can be understood, since it is philosophically unthinkable; perhaps it can only be "glimpsed." (Mullarkey, 2006, 150) All told, grappling with Laruelle's non-philosophy requires the suspension of many of our closely held philosophical assumptions to appreciate his approach to victims and intellectuals.

The Dominant Intellectual

Laruelle presents a portrait of the dominant intellectual in an early chapter of *Intellectuals and Power*. He sees the dominant intellectual as someone who takes up the controlling power of philosophy to the detriment of victims, and in so doing actually sublimates philosophy. In Laruelle's view, the dominant intellectual proceeds from certain philosophical basis, such as "a cause," or "better still, a principal affect," that is contingent on division and opposition. In so doing the dominant intellectual relegates philosophy to the background, where it is exercised in the forms of mediation and mediatized (Laruelle 2015a, 54). According to Laruelle, the "primacy of division, which signals the intellectual's abstract character," is manifested empirically and historically and is marked by ideological features. The dominant intellectual acts, clarifies, analyzes, and resolves ambiguity to reveal the truth. In placing the abstract principle of justice as the dominant value in their defense of victims, dominant intellectuals displace the ultimate end of philosophy, the human. (ibid., 55) In Laruelle's view, such intellectuals also err in the way they adopt other values and causes, such as human rights and the environment, by treating them as absolutes. To be sure, Laruelle is not the first to be critical of the economy of intellectuals. Consider Raymond Aron's critique in *The Opium of the Intellectuals*, a 1955 publication Laruelle cites. Aron did not spare the proletariat, the revolutionary, or the reactionary as he dissected the ideologies that imprisoned them in their lofty positions that were cut off from consequences. For Aron, a little skepticism would go a long way to keep politically inspired intellectuals from falling prey to fanaticism and mythologies. Like Aron, Laruelle finds fault with traditional intellectuals of all stripes—conservative, liberal, and revolutionary (including Marxists)—and claims for himself a nonpartisan position without falling into quietism. But even Aron is not spared in Laruelle's broader critique. Laruelle claims that Aron "rests on" sociology without questioning the Enlightenment assumptions in his work.

On Laruelle's account, the dominant intellectual is a garden-variety ideologue who "considers existence to be like a theatre, which comes to him from the farthest ends of philosophy." (Laruelle 2015a, 67) Such an intellectual thus carries out his mission as if it were a drama played out between himself and the victims he serves. He acts as a self-appointed mediator of history who needs "to inscribe his action within a public space and time…(as an) exhibition." (ibid.) Here, Laruelle is especially critical of dominant intellectuals who capitalize on the media to act out their drama. These "media intellectuals" make their appearances with victims in newspapers, voice their indignation on televised interviews, and express their moral platitudes in opinion columns. But their actions serve only to reinscribe victims in public discourse, without meaningful thought or examination. By itself, media attention does nothing to reveal victims' reality. In the current information age, victims are both seen and unseen—i.e., they are widely exposed in cyberspace, but never properly understood from a non-philosophical perspective. Media intellectuals, Bernard-Henri Lévy among them, exploit media power to buttress their own visibility in the public domain, and in so doing they end up exploiting the very victims they seek to serve. In Laruelle's assessment, a media intellectual is nothing more than a publicity hound, a "super victimizing machine," who "produces opinion for opinion." (2015a, 139)

Indeed, Laruelle questions the effectiveness of the dominant intellectuals' efforts in serving victims. He contends that intellectuals generally see their role as mediators where conflicts arise and work to promote small "provisional peace" between adversaries. The problem, says Laruelle, is that they do so without questioning how their actions might reinscribe power at the next level. Despite good intentions, Laruelle believes that they succeed only in recording and redistributing the ills of society, locking victims in a web of persecution. In this way, intellectuals unwittingly "relay exploitation and universalize it in struggling locally against it—this appearance is their true object." (Ibid., 62) Their work only serves to perpetuate an inescapable circle of injustice in the name of justice.

Laruelle's staunch critique of dominant intellectuals should not be taken as an endorsement of political apathy. While he believes that political engagement is an important aspect of being in the world, he is suspicious of the drawing up of sides by intellectuals in an exercise that can only reinscribe injustice. Laruelle turns to his reading of Foucault to clarify his own position. In a famous conversation between Foucault and Deleuze, Foucault offers a critique of the very notion of "speaking for others," and describes a change in which the masses, who are no longer depend on the intellectual for knowledge, are able to speak for themselves. (Foucault 1977) For Laruelle, this challenges the traditional relationship between victims and intellectuals, as it reconfigures the intellectual/victim dyad in a fundamental way. Laruelle embraces the non-totalizing theory that Foucault offers. Foucault claims that, in a capitalist system, the goal of the politically engaged intellectual is to expose hidden political relationships. "The intellectual's role is no longer to place himself 'somewhat ahead and to the side' in order to express the stifled truth of the collectivity; rather it is to struggle against the forms of power that transform him into its object and instrument in the sphere of 'knowledge,' 'truth,' 'consciousness' and 'discourse'" (Foucault 1977, 208) For Foucault as it is for Laruelle, the point is not conscious-raising for the liberation of the oppressed who depend on intellectuals for this knowledge, but rather the seizing of power alongside of the oppressed.

Sartre's "Plea for Intellectuals"

While Laruelle is critical of media pundits who resemble what Sartre might call engaged intellectuals, elements of Laruelle's and Foucault's position on the role of intellectuals can be found in Sartre's work on the subject, written a few years before. In his Prologue to *Intellectuals and Power*, Petit remarks that not much has been published on public intellectuals since Sartre. Laruelle believes what is needed now is a new theory on intellectuals from a non-philosophical approach. To assess this claim it is important to examine here Sartre's position on the responsibility of intellectuals.

Sartre's portrayal of the committed writer, his idea of an intellectual *par excellence*, is found in a series of essays that were first published in 1947, under the title, *What is Literature?* In this work, Sartre maintains that there is a special responsibility that comes with the privilege of writing for an audience. Specifically, the writer has a responsibility to remain authentic, both to one's audience and to oneself. Authenticity demands that the writer discloses the world truthfully so as to reveal its many contradictions. It is by revealing such contradictions that the writer can take a decisive stance against quietism by committing oneself—and inviting others to commit likewise—to the collaborative task of creating a more open future for all. The authentic intellectual must also strive vigilantly to be reflective and critical of one's own role in promoting social change. Ultimately, the goal of the committed writer is to forge a mutual bond with the audience in what could best be described as a *mitsein* or "we-subject," a reciprocal relationship that at once affirms the freedom of the writer and the freedom of the reader. In this *mitsein*, the reader recognizes the writer as a free subject seeking to represent reality with integrity and from a particular lived experience, while the writer, whose work aims authentically at engaging the reader in dialogue, recognizes the reader's subjectivity as interpreter and respondent to what is being represented.

Sartre would revisit this notion of the committed intellectual in a series of lectures he delivered in Japan in 1965, subsequently published as "A Plea for Intellectuals," and also in an interview he gave after the events of May 1968, published under the title, "A Friend of the People." In both publications, Sartre has remained faithful to his earlier sketch of the responsible writer, while incorporating into that sketch crucial elements that marked his philosophical turn toward Marxism and his political involvement in key events of the period.

In "A Plea for Intellectuals" Sartre begins by distinguishing the true intellectual from its many poor substitutes throughout history. He observes that, up until the 14th Century, French clerics, who had something of a monopoly on knowledge, were guardians of a "sacred ideology" (Sartre, 1976a, 234) that was in reality a "totalitarian myth" designed to preserve the Church's dominant position in the existing social hierarchy (Ibid., 233). The cleric was eventually displaced by a rising class of specialists who were called upon to create an "ideological complex" that served to validate the beliefs and values of the very class into which they were born; namely, the bourgeoisie. By articulating the objective spirit of their own class, the *philosophes*, i.e., the privileged "organic intellectuals" of the Enlightenment, could only advocate a "bourgeois humanism" (Ibid., 236) that fell neatly in line with capitalist ideology.

Sartre then identifies in contemporary society various "technicians of knowledge," a group of highly educated experts and professionals who are mostly recruited from the middle class, and whose function is to deploy their specialized knowledge to advance the current system. In so far as their work serves to maintain the status quo, these technicians act, albeit unwittingly in many cases, as transmitters of established values and custodians of tradition. Sartre maintains that technicians who are content to embrace the dominant ideology exist "in a state of wholly bad faith" (Ibid., 244). They not true intellectuals in his mind. However, if a technician

> becomes aware of the particularism of his ideology and cannot reconcile himself to it; if he sees that he has interiorized authoritarian principles in the form of self-censorship; (…) if he refuses to be a subaltern agent of bourgeois hegemony… then the agent of practical knowledge becomes a monster, that is to say, an intellectual;

someone who attends to what concerns him (…) and whom others refer to a man who interferes in what does not concern him. (Ibid., original italics)

Here Sartre invokes his earlier image of the committed writer who is thoroughly engaged in the world, a disquieting "monster" who, out of concern for others, openly challenges the official capitalist ideology that perpetuates injustice against the oppressed. Modern-day intellectuals, says Sartre, are born of class conflict. Imbued with humanist values, these technicians subscribe to the belief that all people are equal. And yet they are acutely aware of the privileged existence they enjoy, one that stands in stark contradiction with the deprivation of the underclass (Ibid., 239). Reality betrays their sense of humanist egalitarianism. Sartre further infers that the technicians experience a deeper tension here. On the one hand, they know that they ought to renounce their privilege. But since they are themselves the product of this privilege, they cannot renounce their privilege without undoing themselves, which works against their natural instinct toward self-preservation (Ibid., 240).

Furthermore, Sartre contends that all technicians, as professional seekers of knowledge, are defined by what he describes as a fundamental contradiction between professional universalism and class particularism (Ibid., 245). Technicians live with a penetrating tension between universalizing knowledge and particularizing ideology. Their work, despite its purported universality, serves only the particular interests of the dominant class. Sartre gives the example of physicians to illustrate this point. As scientists, doctors endeavor to establish universal forms of knowledge and practice. Their quest for a cure for cancer is intended to serve the common good because it has the potential to cure not just any particular person, but all patients in the global community who are afflicted with the disease. But in reality, doctors find themselves in an elitist system that is controlled by bourgeois ideology and driven by profit. Any remedy they discover becomes a rare commodity accessible only to a privileged few in affluent developed countries. Even as they deny, in the name of objectivity and freedom, that there is such a thing as "bourgeois science," they know all too well that their research is undeniably bourgeois and thus particularist in character and practice. They can see that they are effectively agents of the same ruling class that had produced them, which runs contrary to their mission as universal humanists. What's more, this realization stirs up in them a profound inner conflict. "In as much as their specialty is always the universal," Sartre argues, technicians of knowledge "embody a contestation of the very particularisms with which they have been injected and which they cannot contest without contesting themselves"

(Ibid., 242). This leads Sartre to conclude that technicians are the living embodiment of what Hegel called "unhappy consciousness" (Ibid., 243).

It is this unhappy consciousness that transforms some technicians of knowledge into intellectuals. True intellectuals understand that they cannot confront the particularism of the ruling ideology without also confronting themselves as products, guardians, and beneficiaries of that ideology. And they do so at great existential cost, by engaging in honest self-investigations that call their entire existence into question. Indeed, it is not possible for them to transform themselves without eradicating the contradictions that formed their very selves. Thus intellectuals have before them the first necessary task of liberating themselves from oppressive thoughts, attitudes, and sentiments that had been inculcated in them by the dominant ideology. That is to say, they must "relentlessly combat their own class" (Ibid., 249). This cannot be achieved simply by denouncing bourgeois ideology with rational arguments, but more importantly by committing themselves to the unending process of examining and reexamining their own values and actions to root out any trace of bourgeois particularism. This is true, for example, of the impetus to combat the imperial ideology of racism. As Sartre explains,

> racism is a concrete everyday attitude, and consequently a man can sincerely hold anti-racist opinions of a universal type, while in his deepest recesses, under the influence of his childhood, he remains a racist—so that one day he will involuntarily behave like one in ordinary life. Thus the intellectual's labor will come to nothing, even if he demonstrates the aberrant character of racism, unless he constantly returns to himself to liquidate the traces of racism within him left over by his childhood, by a rigorous investigation of the 'incomparable monster' that is his self. (Ibid., 249)

It is through vigilant self-investigations that intellectuals can achieve the self-awareness needed to transition from being guardians of the status quo to becoming guardians of the "fundamental end," which Sartre defines as "the emancipation, universalization, and hence humanization of man (Ibid., 266)." To distance themselves from the dominant ideology, intellectuals must also situate themselves among the very people whose existence bears witness to the inherent contradictions of that ideology (Ibid., 256). In other words, they must position themselves alongside society's most deprived, in an effort to learn their language and adopt their point of view. Here, Sartre is careful to stress that it is not the intellectuals' place to speak for the underclass. In his mind, not only are the masses capable of self-representation, but the fundamental end of which he speaks cannot be achieved without the masses' direct involvement at every level. Speaking of the importance of the collective voices of the intellectuals and the masses, Sartre opines,

> a newspaper today that is created for the masses should comprise a certain proportion of intellectuals and a certain proportion of workers, and that the articles should be written neither by the intellectuals nor by the workers, but by both together. The workers explain what they are and what they are doing, and the intellectuals are there to understand, to learn, and at the same time to give things every so often a certain type of generalization (Sartre, 1976b, 294).

Putting themselves at the service of the masses, intellectuals should make use of the knowledge and techniques they have acquired, to work for causes that are "genuinely universal," such as "the right of a people to determine its own future." (Ibid., 289) Far from advocating a paternalistic agenda that certifies intellectuals as leaders speaking and deciding for the less fortunate, Sartre insists that true "intellectuals must learn to understand the universal that the masses want, in reality, in the immediate, in this very moment" (Ibid., 294). Sartre ends his plea by returning to familiar themes from his earlier works. Intellectuals "must understand that they cannot liberate themselves unless others are liberated" (Sartre, 1976a, 255). Ultimately, intellectuals are the self-aware technicians of knowledge who choose to walk in solidarity with the masses, with the hope that, as a community of we-subjects, they may bring about their freely chosen ends.

Victims and Generic Intellectuals

Laruelle positions his critique of intellectuals within a broad theory of human beings, one that privileges victims who, he insists, have long been forgotten by philosophy. In his view, philosophy has been more interested in defending of its own power and dominance than in defending victims. By contrast, a non-philosophical theory of intellectuals and victims is non-authoritarian and victim-centered. Here, Laruelle invites us to imagine an intellectual whose "object was no longer justice, truth or other abstract values, but only the victim as the 'real' content of these values" (2015a, 5). This marks the emergence of the determined or generic intellectual, a concept Laruelle developed in *Intellectuals and Power* and *General Theory of Victims*. In both works, Laruelle contrasts the dominant intellectual (what Sartre calls the false intellectual) with the determined intellectual, i.e., one who is determined by the victim. In *Victims*, the latter is replaced by the term generic intellectual. Under Laruelle's non-philosophical approach, the traditional treatment of the power relation between intellectuals and victims is reversed, such that intellectuals are seen as contingent on and characterized by victims. He seeks to situate the "figure of the intellectual of a kind that no longer rises up from spontaneity, in the Nietzschean or Foucauldian sense of the pleb, nor from the consciousness of an avant garde illuminating what remains of the proletariat" (ibid., 57).

According to Laruelle, determined intellectuals occupy a new "sphere" of "intellectual existence" in the world (ibid, 111). What differentiates the determined intellectual from a dominant one is that the former does "victim thinking" without assuming a position of power as a "philosopher of the Victim." The determined intellectual "is thrown into the victims" in a Heideggerian sense, but is not "in the midst of victims." (2015a, 107) This intellectual is not a spokesperson or representative of victims but a "witness cloned from victims by the Victim-in-person," who does not assign ethical values a priori but allows such values to "determine themselves according to the true reality of these victims" (ibid, 142). In the new sphere of victim-thinking, the determined or generic intellectual sees victims directly "in-person," as it were, as a person apart from representations that overdetermine them as the persecuted, the powerless, the enslaved, and the like. This non-philosophical approach to understanding the victim as Victim-in-person effectively transforms the relation between intellectuals and victims, and correspondingly, the role of the intellectual vis-a-vis the victim.

For Laruelle, Victim-in person is an important concept, for it is that through which humanity as such can be understood. He describes victims in general terms as those "without-life lived experiences, the *Erlebnisse* rather than the categories of individuals," and "the non-individual lived experiences of the being-exploited, of the being-excluded, those of the being-murdered, of the being-persecuted, of the being-humiliated." (2015b, 26) Ultimately, "the victim is the condition that under-determines the intellectual to act without claiming to be able to define or determine who is a victim." (ibid., 63) Laruelle thus rejects any notion of an absolute Victim-in-itself, in favor of generic victims who exist pre-predicatively prior to thought or representation, allowing us to "comprehend what we mean by generic man, this of-the-last-instance essence of humans." (ibid., 62) This notion of determination in the last instance, originally attributed to Marx and Engels for historical materialism, now has a Laruellean connotation. The intellectual needs the victim not for self-aggrandisement but rather as the way to understand the Real. The intellectual must be defined in relation to the victim and be underdetermined by the victim in a way that avoids ideology.

It is important to stress that Laruelle sees Victim-in-person as an aspect of the Human-in-person. The latter refers to the undefined person-without-attributes who is neither a psychological nor a political subject but an effect of the Real in-the-last-instance, and real though non-existent.[2] The Victim-in-person is a formal symbol for the most concrete human subject insofar as it "*sustains* a relation to the world" (2015b, 24). And as a formal symbol it captures all positions of victims while remaining indifferent to specific actions and historical moments. Put differently, it is that which determines humanity in the last instance, yet it is not represented in any specific way. Laruelle aims at theorizing about unsung, unrepresented human suffering that are too often eclipsed by lofty ideals and causes that crusaders champion. In the end, he offers a non-philosophical theory that avoids building any profile of victims, constructing any victim types, and, of course, providing any conceptual hierarchy of victim. This explains why present-day victims and their concrete circumstances go unmentioned in his work. For example, consider the homeless person who poses a quandary for the dominant intellectual by refusing to be taken care of by the city. Which is better in this situation-- autonomy or paternalism? Laruelle acknowledges that philosophy can defend both positions. And yet a non-philosophical approach reveals the determined intellectual as one who sees the "initially forced hand (the presupposed Real) and not a final one ... But one that is, at the same time, as if void of determination." (2015a, 88) In part, this is because the determined intellectual is not thinking about the welfare of specific homeless persons, but rather the welfare of humanity as such. Such an intellectual is interested in understanding the possibility that homelessness presents beyond the historical moment, a possibility of disenfranchisement rather than unity of humanity.

Laruelle laments that traditional philosophy will always overlook the reality of the Victim-in-person. Consider an example provided by John O'Maoilearca:

> The prostitute (in Mumbai, or anywhere else) cannot be seen for herself in person, by philosophy. As radical poor or victim-in-person, she resists and is indifferent to the philosophical lens. In any case, philosophy always holds the camera and cast itself in the main role, the image of the Perfect Human in the center of every shot even when it is apparently looking at victims. As non-philosopher, though, Laruelle has always been 'on the side' of the fallen (including 'fallen women'), the unrecorded victims and outcasts. This is not because he is their supposed spokesman or representative but because of the orientation of non-philosophical thought, which is cameraless and begins from their 'side' by default. (O'Maoilearca 2015, 94)

---

[2] The translator actually uses "Man-in-person" which we have challenged for obvious reasons.

The determined or generic intellectual must engage in an *a priori defense* of humanity. This can be done only through a non-philosophical lens, with its inventiveness and its openness in understanding humanity. Laruelle challenges intellectuals to understand the possibility of victimization outside of the Hegelian master/slave dialectic. It is important for them to avoid philosophy's reappropriation of victims within a circular logic of victims and their prosecutors, where the terms, victim and executioner, can be reversible in a sort of "reciprocal approximation of the Victim or executioner" (2015a, 78). Laruelle refers to Sartre here, contending that "this proximity is a problem that the philosophers are unable not to put forward. I think that Sartre has put it forward through the gaze. The gaze, but not only the gaze, is a mode of victimological distance." (ibid.) In non-philosophy, the relationship between generic intellectuals and the Victim-in-person allows for victims to determine their own meaning between representation and non-representation. It is a relationship in which the intellectuals understand that their cause is not history or society, making it possible for them "to carry on a certain emancipatory or liberatory relation to history and society (in relation to philosophy and to the State reunited as a thought-world)." (2015a, 10) To see this point, we must keep in mind that, for Laruelle, humanity is not reducible to a subject and its relations. As Joshua Ramey puts it, persecution is part of a

> continuous revolt against a World whose most basic form of violence consists in the utterly banal attempt to relate or correlate every struggle, need, or concern to a struggle, need, or concern within the World. ... (But in non-philosophy,) the human struggle is a struggle precisely because it is not the struggle of the World, but separate from the World, in the last instance. (Ramey 2012, 84)

Unlike dominant intellectuals who "believe in all-history, in all-politics," and for whom the "specific object, the World, is carried, transported, by historical circumstances and situations," determined intellectuals are underdetermined by history as they refuse to construe humanity merely as a part of history. (2015a, 116) Likewise, as an aspect of Human-in-person, Victim-in-person is not trapped in history but is outside of history since its *a priori* nature is apart from the world. While it is an aspect of the Human-in-person, humanity is not contingent on victimization although it remains a permanent possibility for everyone. (Laruelle, 2015b, 125) This leads Laruelle to conclude that determined or generic intellectuals, who are aware of the seductive power of philosophy, have the task of comprehending victims through a radical understanding of humanity outside of philosophy.

Insurrection

Laruelle summarizes the difference between the victim and the Victim-in-person in this way: "the represented victim causes us to think; the Victim-in-person forces thought or makes us think it as a force without providing the means to think with." (2015a, 138) How then should non-philosophy theorize about victims? Laruelle provides no political strategy here. Moreover, in rejecting philosophy, he has done away with the usual philosophical assumptions about the human being, about human nature and human essence. Indeed, he is even suspicious of philosophies of history. He has effectively excluded all of the usual tools that would guide us in thinking *about* victims, though he would correct us and urge us to *think with* or think *according to* the Real. Laruelle insists that the reality of victims lies in the fact that all humans can be persecuted and that insurrection is possible. In fact, the proper role of the intellectual is to assist victims to become "ordinary messiahs" who can bring about an insurrectional future world with new possibilities for justice. Oddly, the idea of insurrection, which Laruelle invokes in the very subtitle of *Intellectuals and Power*, has only a single reference in that text, appearing near the end in a discussion of the demand for justice. There Laruelle insists that a "society conscious of crime" needs a "new critique of intellectual reason." (2015a, 132) That is to say, a non-standard philosophy is needed to rethink the traditional approach that divides humanity into an opposition between criminals and victims.

In *Victims*, Laruelle again stresses the importance of generic intellectuals to be part of the process to bring about an insurrection, but that they must do so without over-determining victims, as philosophy has done by representing victims as hostages locked in dialectical relationships (e.g., crime and punishment, masters and slaves, oppressors and oppressed). Laruelle also faults the engaged intellectual's inclination to classifying victims under specific labels (e.g., survivors, evil-sufferers, casualties of crimes against humanity, etc.). It is the generic intellectual who avoids any determinant representation of victims and engages in the process of "generically merging or superposing himself with the victim for an experience that will not be a new contemplation but a unique knowledge that inextricably holds for both the victim and himself." (2015b, 55) In Laruelle's view, media intellectuals have confused "superposition with identification." The unique knowledge produced by superposition with victims is important because, after all, intellectuals can also be victims in so far as the Victim-in-person is an aspect of the Human-in-person. Just as the human-in-person, as a clone of the Real, is not any particular subject produced by philosophical discourse, the victim-in-person likewise is not any individuated victim represented by any particular category, space, or time. This is again Laruelle's way of negating any notion of an absolute victim in itself.

Keeping in mind that generic intellectuals do not think of victims representationally as particular subjects, but rather according-to the Victim-in-person as part of humanity in general, Laruelle maintains that the proper relationship of intellectuals to victims is compassion. Compassion is what allows the intellectual and the victim to share in the suffering of all people, without reducing either one to victimhood. It is in this sense that Laruelle speaks of compassion as insurrection. As he puts it, compassion is "the fusion" in "non-representative space" of the victim and "the thought attached to it. … (It is a fusion) through a collision of the essentially generic victim and the essentially philosophical intellectual in the Victim-in-person." (2015b, 114). Here, Laruelle draws a sharp contrast between compassion and pity. Whereas in compassion the intellectual operates in fusion with the victim-in person, in pity, the intellectual operates from a position of superiority and power founded on the separation of victims from non-victims. Compassion allows for an ethical assistance to victims that is non-philosophical, a means by which the generic intellectual thinks about humanity in its radical immanence across differences in time and culture. In this way compassion discloses intellectuals as generic victims. As Alexander Galloway puts it, Laruelle is endorsing something of a "mystical maoism" here by insisting "that we are all always already victims, simply by virtue of being human. The problem is not so much victimization itself, but the decision to divide the world into victims and not." (Galloway 2013, 103)

Laruelle's non-philosophical approach to understanding intellectuals and victims ushers in a new, "non-standard" ethics for humanity. Though justice is necessary, Laruelle avoids all absolutes and refrains from representing justice empirically or historically. By refusing all oppositions, all divisions, and all power relations, Laruelle places both intellectuals and victims back in humanity in its radically indeterminate form. Ethics begins with the generic victim that is none of us and all of us. Under this new ethics the proper role of the intellectual is to assist in the victims' uprising by fusing with the Victim-in-person in compassion and care. By superpositioning with the victim, the generic intellectual recognizes the victim as under-determining and produces knowledge of the victim's uprising through this recognition. It is the victim's task to discern the demand for justice, and the intellectual's task provisionally to think through the content, goals, and values of political engagement (e.g. justice, globalization, equality), all the while positioning the Victim-in-person as the "under-determining condition of justice." (2015b, xx) Whereas Laurelle believes in a "true uprising of victims" that can under-determine the crime and the criminal, he cautions that it must be "taken up and revived by the intellectual compelled to a future-thought." (2015b, 130) His hope here is that the transformation of the intellectual to a generic, future-oriented intellectual will be transformative for society, history and philosophy. The future intellectual recognizes that the Human-in-person does not allow classification of victims, for victims on the generic level are unrepresentable and therefore resist victimhood.

Conclusion

Laruelle's recent work on victims is an important contribution in post-continental thought, one that disrupts a trajectory for thinking about the philosophical intellectual, a trajectory that began with a plea from the last century's most celebrated example. Laruelle answers Sartre's "Plea" by raising the stakes. Rather than championing the oppressed by shining a bright light on criminals, executioners, murderous butchers, tyrants, corrupt regimes and the like, Laruelle calls upon us first to inspect philosophy itself, its limits, its tyrannical use of power, as well as the ways in which intellectuals, in serving philosophy, betray victims. Laruelle's theory of victims, which focuses on humanity in-the-last-instance, is non-political in so far as it represents non-philosophy. His notions of Human-in-person and Victim-in-person are non-binary, non-oppositional and non-authoritarian.

Reading Sartre after Laruelle, it is tempting to ask how close Sartre comes to being what Laruelle describes as a generic intellectual. To what extent is Sartre's "Plea" one that comes from the future? Sartre always dared to imagine a classless society, one that was thoroughly egalitarian and devoid of hierarchies of all sorts. In his later writings, Sartre shows himself to be much closer to a generic intellectual in the Laruellean sense. There we find Sartre seeking a philosophy of history, a path forward after Marxism, and theorizing about a conception of human fraternity without division through the notion of the "*we*" in *Hope Now*. Indeed, we find a resolute Sartre trying to escape the bondage of philosophy and ontology, and casting doubt on the relevance of the intellectual *qua* intellectual while remaining politically committed. It is interesting to trace the evolution of the 'we' in Sartre. There are hints that he has moved from a dialectical model in *Being and Nothingness* to a conflict model in the *Critique*, and finally to a non-totalizing conception of fraternity in *Hope Now*. At the very end of his life, Sartre, while struggling to imagine something better than a competitive model of human relationships marked by violence and terror, would define the 'we' or 'community' simply as "a body of people who struggle as one." (Sartre 1996, 67) If we take this definition as representing Sartre's third ethics, it would appear to be one that comes close to a Laruellean post-totalizing, non-hierarchical and non-authoritarian understanding of the generic human community, even though the notions of 'Human-in-person' and 'in-the-last instance' are obviously missing in Sartre. The question of how such a human community based on reciprocity would come to pass is left largely unaddressed in both Laruelle and Sartre. To be sure, Sartre would argue that the communal relations among human beings that he envisioned will not emerge out of a mere conceptualization of fraternity by intellectuals, but will require a real change in historical conditions. Ultimately, Laruelle and Sartre have merely shown that what is needed is a different view of philosophy (or non-philosophy) of history.

Laurelle, for his part, refuses the role of public intellectual, while preferring to stay in the non-philosophical trenches. In doing so, he leaves aside the pressing question of our ethical obligations to others, one that has remained a central concern for Sartre. We see this in his quick dismissal of Sartre during his interview with Petit, when Petit reminds him of Sartre's famous comment on the limits of literature in confronting the evils of starvation. "In the face of a dying child," Sartre acknowledges, "*Nausea* has no weight." (Sartre, 1965, 13) In prioritizing survival in this remark, Sartre admits to a progression in his own thinking. As he confesses, "I have served a slow apprenticeship to the real. I have seen children starving to death." (Ibid.) Such comments fail to impress Laruelle, however, who considers these examples as an "overwhelming and intimidating abstraction, almost a sin against children and against literature." (Laruelle 2015a, 70) Rather than a "universal obsession with survival," which the recent refugee crisis and acts of terrorism in France might proffer, Laruelle opts for a non-humanitarian path, allowing "only impossible definitions of the Victim." In this dust-up with Sartre, indirect though it is, we see the daylight between them. Laruelle does not dismiss Sartrean activism; he sees a role for politics and political action but deliberately avoids offering any comprehensive political philosophy. Instead, Laruelle points to a path forward that holds in tension a riveting focus on (undefinable) victims (presently an inescapable condition of humanity), while also theorizing about the Human-in-person, an abstraction. Preempting the inevitable demand for an ethics, he introduces a non-standard ethics that offers a view of compassion, and relies on the radical non-action of unpower through the superposition of intellectuals with victims. His general theory will incite no revolts by victims, save for one – a possible revolt against doing a certain kind of philosophy. It is a bold call to inventing a truly non-authoritarian intellectual practice, even as critics might render that an impossible task.

Laruelle's work on victims suggests what it might mean for non-philosophy to have a preference for the destitute, for the least privileged in global society. The fleeting glances in media coverage of widespread disasters that such people suffer provide a starting point for the work of future-oriented intellectuals.

Prof. Dr. Constance L. Mui, Loyola University New Orleans, USA, cmui[at]loyno.edu
Prof. Dr. Julien S. Murphy, College of Arts and Sciences, University of Southern Maine,
Portland ME, USA, jmurphy[at]maine.edu

References

Anderson, Taylor W. "On 2017's Darkest Day, Utahns Gather to Mourn the 117 Homeless and Formerly Homeless People Who Died this Year," The Salt Lake Tribune, December 22, 2017, <http://www.sltrib.com/news/politics/2017/12/22/on-2017s-darkest-day-utahns-gather-to-mourn-the-117-homeless-and-formerly-homeless-people-who-died-this-year/>.

Aron, Raymond. *The Opium of the Intellectuals*. Translated by Terence Kilmartin and Lucile Brockway, New York: W.W. Norton and Company, 1962.

Belson, Ken and Jennifer Medina and Richard Pérez-Peña. "A Burst of Gunfire, a Pause, Then Carnage in Las Vegas That Would Not Stop." *The New York Times* October 2, 2017, <https://www.nytimes.com/2017/10/02/us/las-vegas-shooting-live-updates.html?_r=0>.

Brassier, Ray. *Nihil Unbound: Enlightenment and Extinction*. New York: Palgrave Macmillan Press, 2007.

Burk, Drew S. *François Laruelle: Struggle and Utopia At The End Times of Philosophy*. Translated by Drew S. Burk and Anthony Paul Smith, Minneapolis: Univocal Press, 2012.

Foucault, Michel. "Intellectuals and Power: A Conversation between Michel Foucault and Giles Deleuze," in Donald F. Bouchard (ed.) *Language, Counter-Memory, Practice: Selected Essays and Interviews by Michel Foucault*. Translated by Bouchard and Sherry Simon, Ithaca: Cornell University Press, 1977, 205-217.

Galloway, Alexander R. "François Laruelle, *Théorie générale des victimes*." Review. *Parrhesia* 16, (2013), 102-105.

Gangle, Rocco. *François Laruelle's Philosophies of Difference: A Critical Introduction and Guide.* Edinburgh: Edinburgh University Press, 2013.

Henry, Michel. *Material Phenomenology.* Translated by S. Davidson, New York: Fordham University Press, 2008.

Hoey, Dennis. "Vigil in Portland to Honor 37 Homeless People Who Died this Year," December 18, 2017, *Portland Press Herald,* <http://www.pressherald.com/2017/12/18/vigil-in-portland-to-honor-37-homeless-people-who-died-this-year/>.

Koehn, Alexandra. Highest Number of Homeless Deaths Recorded in 2017, News Channel 5 Network, Dec. 16, 2017, <https://www.newschannel5.com/news/highest-number-of-homeless-deaths-recorded-in-2017>.

Laruelle, François. "Non-Philosophy, Weapon of Last Defence: An Interview with François Laruelle," translated by Anthony Paul Smith, in Mullarkey, John and Anthony Paul Smith (eds.). *Laruelle and Non-Philosophy.* Edinburgh: Edinburgh University Press, 2012, 238-251.

Laruelle, François (in conversation with Philippe Petit). *Intellectuals and Power: The Insurrection of the Victim.* Translated by Anthony Paul Smith. Cambridge: Polity Press, 2015a.

Laruelle, François. *General Theory of Victims.* Translated by Jessie Hock and Alex Dubilet. Malden, MA: Polity Press, 2015b.

Luppi, Kathleen. "Candlelight Memorial Honors O.C. Homeless People Who Died This Year," *Los Angeles Times*, December 22, 2017, <http://www.latimes.com/socal/daily-pilot/entertainment/tn-wknd-et-homeless-memorial-20171222-story.html>.

Merleau-Ponty, Maurice. "Philosophy and Non-Philosophy Since Hegel." *Telos* No. 29, (1976): 43-105.

Meyer, Eric D. "*General Theory of Victims.*" Review. *Dialogue* No. 1, (2016): 1-3.

Mullarkey, John. *Post-Continental Philosophy: An Outline.* New York: Continuum Press, 2006.

O' Maoilearca, John. *All Thoughts are Equal, Laruelle and Nonhuman Philosophy.* Minneapolis: University of Minnesota Press, 2015.

Ramey, Joshua. "The Justice of Non-Philosophy," in John Mullarkey and Anthony Paul Smith (eds.) *Laurelle and Non-Philosophy.* Edinburgh: Edinburgh University Press, 2012.

Sartre, Jean-Paul, "Sartre's explique sur *Les Mots.*" Interview with Jacqueline Piatier, *Le Monde,* 18, April, 1965.

Sartre, Jean-Paul, "A Plea for Intellectuals," in Jean-Paul Sartre. *Between Existentialism and Marxism.* New York: William Morrow, 1976, 228-285.

Sartre, Jean-Paul, "A Friend of the People," in Jean-Paul Sartre. *Between Existentialism and Marxism.* New York: William Morrow, 1976, 286-298.

Sartre, Jean-Paul. *What is Literature and Other Essays.* Cambridge: Harvard University Press, 1988.

Sartre, Jean-Paul and Benny Lévy. *Hope Now: The 1980 Interviews*. Translated by Adrian Van Den Hoven. Chicago: University of Chicago Press, 1996.

Walsh, Declan and Nour Youssef, "Militants Kill 305 at Sufi Mosque in Egypt's Deadliest Terrorist Attack," November 24, 2017, *The New York Times*, <https://www.nytimes.com/2017/11/24/world/middleeast/mosque-attack-egypt.html>

KATERINA KOLOZOVA (Skopje)

Philosophy as capitalism and the socialist radically metaphysical response to it

Abstract

The author starts from the thesis that there is no such thing as a "natural" or "apolitical" economy. The economy is always already political, as it is the economy's material core of power, control, and its main mechanisms, i.e. exploitation and oppression. It is no less so in the era of neoliberalism, a time in which we witness the divorce between capitalism and democracy. In order to lay the foundations of a different economy, one that is not based on wage labor and the exploitation of human life and nature based on their auto-alienation, but rather on action in accordance with their resources, we need – according to the author – to rethink the concept of the state in a non-philosophical and post-capitalist fashion, structurally different from the modern bourgeois state. If the structure originating in the bourgeois state, as conceived by modern humanism, is preserved, it will mean that the determination in the last instance is still the same. In order to arrive at a determination in the last instance of a non-exploitative, non-wage-labor-based social order where the determination is affected by the real, we must first arrive at the generic core of the notion of the modern state. As soon as we determine the generic term of "the state," we can radicalize it by letting it be determined by the effects of the real. The generic notion, isolated from the chôra of the transcendental material that is offered by modern philosophies originating in the Enlightenment, should be used as the minimal transcendental description for the determining effect (or "symptom") of the real.

Keywords: François Laruelle, Karl Marx, capitalism, neoliberalism, state, non-philosophy

1. The neoliberal state is no weak and naturalness of capitalism if a philosophical phantasm

The organization of social production beyond the principle of private property qua property based on wage labor needs to be conceived in terms of a given historical and material context. There is no single form of commonality, beyond historical context and the real conditions that it generates. Any form of commonality that transcends the praxis of historically determined conditioning circumstances are an abstraction, and idea hovering independently from the material universe. In the first decade of the 21st century, we possess active memory of the reign and demise of "the communist states" of the mid-20th century in Eastern and Central Europe. By inertia, we tend to imagine the state-owned commons of those states as the model of socialist commonality in ownership.

If we submit to the dictate of the real of the material and immaterial conditions of our contemporaneity, the concept of commonality that we would generate would follow the syntax of the real as the conditioning of its possibilities. We live in an era of accelerated capitalism, in capital's "bubbles" and "financial crises," which, as we already tried to demonstrate, exist in an almost parallel fashion to the real economy of the deregulating neoliberal politico-economic doctrine. The alleged deregulation of the neoliberal economy is in fact a product of a meticulous scientifically, ideologically, politically, and technocratically elaborated methodology of control, masquerading as the manifestation of the anarchic natural laws of the free market economy. We live in an era in which states bailout banks with the money collected through taxes paid by wage laborers. The "weak state" of neoliberalism is stronger and more economically disciplining and socially ruthless than any other form of a bourgeois state that we have witnessed in the second half of the 20th century. In addition to the bank bailouts by the state, let us note that "austerity measures" are one of the most prominent features of the post-2008 economy in Europe.

In short, there is no such thing as a natural or apolitical economy. The economy is always already political, as it is the economy's material core of power, control, and its main mechanisms – i.e. exploitation and oppression. It is no less so in the era of neoliberalism, a time in which we witness the divorce between capitalism and democracy. The divorce is scandalous as we see totalitarian states, such as China, Russia, and Turkey as the new economic superpowers, ever more superior to the West, being the EU and the US. Western countries also are executing a split between democracy and capitalism, nonetheless one that is less scandalously ostensible. Their means of state controlled economy, whose policies do not require and moreover prevent the possibility of democratic expression of endorsement or refusal on the part of the citizens, consists in the measures of "austerity cuts," "market oriented education," rising gender and social inequality, and the sacrifice of the basic human freedoms in the name of "security" in an era of "war against terrorism" that has lasted for more than a decade. *To believe the narrative of the weak state overpowered by the elemental forces of capitalism implies a prior belief in the narratives of the naturalness of the economic laws (of capitalism).*

In order to lay the foundations of a different economy, one that is *not* based on wage labor and the exploitation of human life and nature based on their auto-alienation, but rather on action in accordance with their resources, we must rethink the concept of the state in a non-philosophical and post-capitalist fashion, structurally different from the modern bourgeois state. If the structure originating in the bourgeois state, as conceived by modern humanism, is preserved, it will mean that the determination in the last instance is still the same. In order to arrive at a determination in the last instance of a non-exploitative, non-wage-labor-based social order where the determination is affected by the real, we must first arrive at the generic core of the notion of the modern state. As soon as we determine the generic term of "the state," we can radicalize it by letting it be determined by the effects of the real. The generic notion, isolated from the *chôra* of the transcendental material that is offered by modern philosophies originating in the Enlightenment, should be used as the minimal transcendental description for the determining effect (or "symptom") of the real.

2. Auto-acceleration of capitalism as speculation and its political infrastructure

According to Marx in Volume 3 of *Capital*, the inherent laws of the capitalist political and economic order will nourish and exacerbate the contradiction between pure speculation as the primary mode of operation of capitalism and the instance of the material it aims to control and exploit. Speculation out of joint will assume a life of its own, detached from the material possession of capital as private property or as simply having actual money. Speculative capital, the capital with which the finance industry operates today, is potential money, it is projection of value or speculation. Its potentiality derives from investments of mere estimations of the worth of third persons' material property and assets. It is the association of investors and clients, creditors and debtors, the networks they create, and the financial fluxes that such networks navigate, that create financial growth and its economic (side) effects. Marx writes:

> The capital, which in itself rests on a social mode of production and presupposes a social concentration of means of production and labour-power, is here [stock exchange market] directly endowed with the form of social capital (capital of directly associated individuals) as distinct from private capital, and its undertakings assume the form of social undertakings as distinct from private undertakings. It is the abolition of capital as private property within the framework of capitalist production itself. (Marx 1984)

Contemporary finance capital, or the so called finance industry, relies and profits from the operations of circulation as a process *per se* and as tautology, divorced from any grounding in the material basis of capital.

I have explained the process in more detail in the previous pages of this book, not only in theoretical terms, but also in terms of evidence related to the post 2008 crisis in the US and henceforth globally. I also presented data, derived from the US Government commissioned report on the crisis, pointing out the fact that the greatest giants of the finance industry had been operating with virtually no capital investment of their own. Their "capital" had been the information, knowledge, and political empowerment – an engagement of speculation that the US government report on the crisis termed more than once as swindling. (See Financial Crisis Inquiry Commission 2011) According to Marx, such a development is necessary and inevitable as the last stage of capitalism:

> This is the abolition of the capitalist mode of production within the capitalist mode of production itself, and hence a self-dissolving contradiction, which prima facie represents a mere phase of transition to a new form of production. It manifests itself as such a contradiction in its effects. It establishes a monopoly in certain spheres and thereby requires state interference. It reproduces a new financial aristocracy, a new variety of parasites in the shape of promoters, speculators and simply nominal directors; a whole system of swindling and cheating by means of corporation promotion, stock issuance, and stock speculation. It is private production without the control of private property. (Marx 1894)

This stage is metastatic for capitalism, ensuing into the greatest imaginable contradiction that will lead to self-dissolution, says Marx.

Post-2008 finance capitalism is one of perpetual crisis, whereas, as Jacques Rancière says, crisis cannot be a permanent pathological state as, by definition, it is not permanent. Instead, it is the "robust health system" of exploitation presented as illness to the "ignorant ones" or to the exploited (those who can be scientifically convinced that they are "ill" rather than exploited). (Rancière 2014, 13) What our contemporary media and corporate political powers call "crisis" seems to be, by all of its constitutive characteristics, the final stage of capitalism which Marx describes as "self-dissolving." It unveils the reality of economic production and social and technological progress as one unfolding virtually independently from the "material basis" (monetarily re-presented materiality) of private capital.

The acceleration process, which is bound to happen through what Marx called "the credit system," the ever growing distance between actual paying and buying of a commodity, and the possibility of an ever expanding "intermission" of the credit period, divulges the spectrality of capital, money, and private property. Acceleration through the "credit system" as the final stage of capitalism is announced and elaborated by Marx in Volume III, Chapter 5 of *Capital*. As the US Government Report on the 2008 financial crisis shows, Wall Street CEO's do not have to invest any *real* or *actual* private property, and practically no capital of theirs has to be invested in order to initiate, manage, and profit from an investment project. Quite the contrary, it is the private property of the poor that had been invested and then defaulted as the post 2007 crisis occurred. By no material investment of one's own, "industrialists" create an unstoppable growing capital that enables them and the government to control society as the highest form of politico-economic power. The illusion of capital's materiality and material property, serving as the basis for an economy, has become apparent through the financial speculation whose final form had become sheer swindling. Albeit aiming at pure profit and exploitation of the poor only, the crisis has also and unwittingly so shown that the "emperor had been naked" for quite some time – that capital as the material and real basis of economic processes is a mirage. On the basis of this particular contradiction, the "stock exchange managers" have managed to amass most of the material resources for themselves.

Acceleration is immanent to capitalism. Capitalism is unstoppably accelerated by the inherent laws of speculation itself, and therefore that of de-materialization.

> On one hand, the acceleration is technical; for example, with the same magnitude and number of actual turnovers of commodities for consumption, a smaller quantity of money or money tokens performs the same service. This is bound up with the technique of banking. On the other hand, credit accelerates the velocity of the metamorphoses of commodities, and thereby the velocity of money circulation. [...] Acceleration by means of credit, of the individual phases of circulation or the metamorphosis of commodities, and later the metamorphosis of capital, and with it an acceleration of the process of reproduction in general. (On the other hand, credit helps to keep the acts of buying and selling apart longer, and serves thereby as a basis for speculation.) Contraction of reserve funds may be viewed in two ways: as a reduction of the circulating medium on the one hand, and on the other, as a reduction of that part of capital which must always exist in the form of money. (Marx 1894)

One does not need the enactment of a "process of acceleration" of capitalism as a form of resistance aimed at its demise, as the "Accelerationist Manifesto" argues, (Williams and Srnicek 2013) simply because it is a process generated by capitalism itself. Acceleration does not only take place in the form of finance capital, but also in the area of material production, i.e., in technological-militaristic development. The unstoppable development of the means of production, which is also the means of exploitation of the human species, is constantly accelerated. This is technological development. Technological development is subject to private property, capital invested in it, and the material conditions for it; its inventions are in the possession of capitalist oligarchs exclusively. The imagined political revolution via technological acceleration requires a reversed model of ownership and reinvention of the social role of technological development. In order to achieve these communist goals, following the model of associations of producers advocated by Marx, the technological processes, which are physically (really or "materially") grounded in the individuals who innovate, should be appropriated by the actual producers. As a consequence, this will lead to a replacement of the spectrality and superfluity of capital (money, derivatives, bitcoin, in all its forms) by real and tangible social re-production, whereby I am reducing production to reproduction and any productive excess is simply that, excess and excess is creativity.

However, politics in the strict sense is far more complex than economics. It enacts the totality of the relations in a society. That is why the new political horizon cannot be reduced to a shift in economic production and ownership. It needs to be invented in accordance with the principle of radical sociality of production as the central economic fundament, as well as with the political (and metaphysical) goal of transcending the dualism of "the belly and the abstract activity." (Marx 1959a)

In capitalism, the product of a social process, i.e. of an "association of producers" of commodities, consists of use value and surplus value, or in the case of the finance industry, of surplus value only. It is claimed as property by a handful of people coordinating the social process, including both the political and the economic reality. In other words, capitalism, in particular in its neoliberal form, is not so much about the material possession of what is potentially capital, but about the capacity and entitlement to assign monetary value, and hence, the status of capital and, for that matter, of commodity as well. This is political capacity and entitlement.

In what Marx announces as the late stage of capitalism, i.e. in finance capitalism, the process of signification – of turning a material, physical good into market value or commodity – is mainly carried out through mere "swindling," as mentioned in the US report on the post 2008 financial crisis. In this process, the "private ownership of property" has been proven to be "just ownership" as Marx predicted – a mere instance of the material to be exploited by the "stock exchange managers" as Marx anticipated in the Third Volume of

Capital. As the essentially speculative nature of the capitalist economy has accelerated, the central contradiction has moved to an extreme. According to Marx, the contradiction taken *in extremis* must be resolved by self-dissolving the impossible, unsustainable, contradicting couple. If the unsustainable and bubbled up speculative aspect of the contradiction culminates, if it exacerbates the fissure with the real and the physical that it has introduced *in principio*, it will founder as the real starts to "act on its own," escaping the control of philosophy (= ideology of capitalism). Unruly as it is, thanks to its brutal, physical force, or/and the force of the real, which can include material actions carried out by inanimate agencies, it will disperse the ruling webs of meaning, or the existing universe and estimation of values. Such a process would lead to the self-dissolution of the founding binary of capitalism, because *the reality is constituted by, grounded in, and conditioned by social process, rather than capital investment (in the form of actual monetary assets)*. Materiality of contemporary reality lies in society, in its physicality and effects of a conditioning real, rather than in the symbolism of money.

3. Reversing the self-dissolving binary

Following Marx's prescriptions, if and when the above takes place, we will be called upon to build a vision of materiality, sociality, and socialism on the material or real basis of the determination in the last instance of the existing and most profitable economic models. This ought to be done by recourse to their materialist revolution, i.e. by way of arriving at the material/physical determination in the last instance of social representation. The goal of such procedure would be to ground the economic models subject to revolutionary reversal in the material qua real, and condition them by it, i.e. by their material determination in the last instance.

This result of the ultimate development of capitalist production is a necessary transitional phase towards the reconversion of capital into the property of producers, although no longer as private property of the individual producers, but rather as the property of associated producers or outright social property. On the other hand, the stock company is a transition towards the conversion of all functions in the reproduction process that still remain linked with capitalist property into mere functions of associated producers, or into social functions.

Divested from any real, material, or physical base, divested from a base that maintains its connection with the material via the proxy of investment capital, the model of production dominated by the finance industry unravels the economy's fundamental sociality. Let us remind ourselves of the US Government's report on the post 2008 financial crisis, which notes and documents that the crisis was provoked by the fact that investment giants were operating with virtually no capital of their own. Investment mortgage backed funds or bank crediting were *de facto* made possible by clients' investments, i.e. assets that were at risk to be defaulted. In line with Marx's vision of the last, most developed, and metastatic stage of capitalism, we will call the latter "mere capital owners" (Marx), whereas the true capitalists are those who "manage" the funds without investing any of their material property. He writes:

> Transformation of the actually functioning capitalist into a mere manager or, administrator of other people's capital, and of the owner of capital into a mere owner, a mere money, is capitalist [sic]. Even if the dividends that which they receive include the interest and the profit of enterprise, i.e., the total profit (for the salary of the manager is, or should be, simply the wage of a specific type of skilled labour, whose price is regulated in the labour-market like that of any other labour), this total profit is henceforth received only in the form of interest, i.e., as mere compensation for owning capital that now is entirely divorced from the function in the actual process of reproduction, just as this function in the person of the manager is divorced from ownership of capital. Profit thus appears (no longer only that portion of it, the interest, which derives its justification from the profit of the borrower) as a mere appropriation of the surplus-labour of others, arising from the conversion of means of production into capital, i.e., from their alienation vis-à-vis the actual producer, from their antithesis as another's property to every individual actually at work in production, from manager down to the last day-labourer. In stock companies the function is divorced from capital ownership, hence also labour is entirely divorced from ownership of means of production and surplus-labour. (Marx 1894)

The Report of the Inquiry Committee on the 2008 financial crisis confirms this projection to be true, and provides ample evidence for it:

> In the years leading up to the crisis, too many financial institutions, as well as too many households, borrowed to the hilt, leaving them vulnerable to financial distress or ruin if the value of their investments declined even modestly. For example, as of 2007, the five major investment banks – Bear Stearns, Goldman Sachs, Lehman Brothers, Merrill Lynch, and Morgan Stanley – were operating with extraordinarily thin capital. By one measure, their leverage ratios were as high as 40 to 1, meaning for

every $40 in assets, there was only $1 in capital to cover losses. (Financial Crisis Inquiry Commission 2011, xix)

Those who capitalize on an investment and those who extract immense profit do not in fact own the material basis for it. What they own is a legally designated status to operate and profit from someone else's private property. Once this becomes obvious, what remains to be done is that someone finally shouts, "the emperor is naked," or at least starts behaving like it. What gives life to the finance industry is the will of "the mere owners of capital" (the exploited ones) to enter into associations that create profit. These processes are fundamentally social. Only a purely social process can enable the usurpation of the real by speculation. In order to overcome the alienation created by such usurpation, which foregrounds exploitation of the bodies of human and non-human animals, one ought to seek the purely material – as the real, physical or practical, and "material," in Marx's sense – grounding of the social.

4. The material or non-speculative grounding of the social

Sociality is a linguistic and communicative reality. Its means are of language. Fundamentally, it is subjectivity. Its radical subjectivity is that which admits the jarring difference between the Laruellian "Stranger," the inevitable gesture of the auto-alienation of the real as the fundament of subjectivity formation, and the real. The radical subjectivity is defined by its anteriority to any philosophical ambition to reconcile the two instances by way of usurping the real, a gesture executed by virtue of establishing an amphibology between the real and the "meaning" (language, subjectivity, truth). Philosophy, regardless of its inner plurality, can be seen as a monolithic phenomenon in the following sense – it inevitably establishes an equation between the real and thought. Even when it declares an insurmountable split between the two, even when it declares the real to be inaccessible, as in the case of the post-Kantian critical legacy, it still thinks in terms of the equation. Namely, by relegating the real into the realm of the unthinkable, the inaccessible to thought, it commits a "fuite en avance (preemptive escape) into fiction" (Laruelle), resulting into instituting language (thought/"fiction"/the Stranger) as the only form of reality that thought should be interested in and aspire to understand. (Laruelle 1989, 231) Thereby, the philosophical affirmation of the irreconcilable split between the real and thought, and of the real's radical indifference to thought's aspirations, remains within the perennial philosophical equation rendering the real reducible to "truth," i.e. to thought. This result is brought about precisely by the reversal of the equation. Namely, through the gesture of declaring the real non-existent, being that it is non-existent for and to us, the philosophical thought of the post-Kantian turn assigns to language the status of the real and perpetuates the same amphibology. (See Kolozova 2014, 1)

Consequently, in order to determine the material grounding of sociality in the last instance, i.e. in order to establish its determination in the last instance as determination in terms of the real, one ought to avoid philosophical circularity of thought. With the aim of achieving this goal, we shall apply the non-philosophical method of arriving to a concept that is radically descriptive, i.e., minimally transcendental in its identification of the effect of the real that determines it in the last instance. (Laruelle 2000, 47) Such posture of thought is fundamentally scientific, argues Laruelle consistently throughout his opus. Scientific thought is primitive and naive insofar as it aims to be descriptively exhaustive but does not institute a "truth" of the real, nor does it deal with its "essence." (Laruelle 2012, 98) Describing exteriority, its locations, its operations, its effects (on the environment, including the humans), and arriving at an elaborate description is what scientific thought aspires to do.

> Philosophy will always look for and posit science too late – at the end of its 'reflection,' at the end of its 'project' of objectivity, at the end of its 'dialectic', and in general at the end of the transcendence that founds all of its techniques. Now, it is precisely transcendence that science excludes, at least from the relation (of non-relation) that it 'maintains' in the last instance with the real. Hence, its naivety, its unreflectiveness, its realism, its 'blindness,' which is so insupportable to philosophical objectification that the latter never stops denigrating them, reducing them, or falsifying them – this is what goes by the name of 'epistemology', and is the very epistemo-logos in every epistemology. (Ibid., 99-100)

To define the "essence" of human existence in philosophical terms is to commit violence against the physical (or the "material" in the Marxist or non-philosophical sense). To place it in the realm of abstraction or "pure value" is to formulate it as a *surplus value*. The philosophical determination in the last instance of the human species is no different from the capitalist one. A materialist determination of the human based on Marx's conception of materialism without philosophy, i.e. "scientific" materialism, is one that views the instance of the mental also materialistically. Therefore, if the fundamental interest of the proletariat is social, the form of sociality that the "communist horizon" postulates as its goal is one that would be materially determined by a sense of wellbeing. It will consist of what Marx calls "spiritual satisfaction," combined and in no contradiction with the bodily. Let us remind ourselves one more time that Marx argues that the true goal of communism is the transcendence of human alienation created by the body/mind dichotomy. (Marx 1959b) The "spiritual" necessarily materializes itself as a bodily sensation:

> That man's physical and spiritual life is linked to nature means simply that nature is linked to itself, for man is a part of nature. (Karl Marx 1959a)

The material that Marx is concerned with is that of the physical, of what can suffer or sense pleasure, or in other words, the material of the organic. In the last instance, praxis is also determined by the physical. The communist emancipation is an emancipation of the physical from the tyranny of Hegel's Spirit detached from and opposed to the material or the real. It can be reduced to the hierarchically superior constituent of the archaic binary of the body and mind, or matter and idea. It also entails emancipation of the spiritual, which suffers from the alienation and the split between the spiritual and physical production. The spiritual suffers insofar as it is an abstract ruling the physical turned into an object, treated as if it was an inanimate matter. It suffers from its own deprivation of physical sensation, of the death of the physical that it contains in order to be an abstraction. Therefore, technological progress and its acceleration, in communist terms, can be emancipating so long as they are emancipating the subjugated physical and nature. A society of emancipated bodies and minds, a society that has transcended the split and hierarchy between the two, can create and sustain an economy based on the "free associations of producers." The communist concept of economy operates only by virtue of suspending the hierarchy of the "higher good" (an abstraction) over the physical, including the "higher good" of communism and its economy of "free associations." As long as they produce the division of "the belly and the abstract activity," they are not communist. (Marx 1959a)

A communist producer is not alienated from his or her work and its fruits. Therefore, in some sense, communism offers a sense of possession or ownership for every member of society. In order for this "sense of possession" to be material, it has to be realized physically through the bodies of the members of the society. Therefore, in order for communism to be communal it also has to be very individualistic, as each *body* in a society must vouch for it. The idea that the individual must suffer in the name of a common good is absurd (from a materialist point of view, meaningless) and one never argued for by Marx. If so, the common good would become a purpose in itself, a self-serving and auto-referential goal. Hence, it would become an abstraction, detached from the physical experiences of the bodies of a society (not the "social body," as that is yet another abstraction).

In short, by the very logic of Marx's argument, the opposition between the individual and the common would be untenable. Also, it is something Marx never argued for. His critique of the private property is historical, and therefore concerns its bourgeois and/or capitalist form. An argument in favor of sacrificing the individual wellbeing in the name of an abstract higher good is one of martyrdom. Martyrdom is a theological and metaphysical value, not a communist one. Communism is radically democratic. The Leninist and post-Leninist legacy of communism has instituted it as a form of Abrahamic theology, of self-sacrifice and sacrifices, of martyrdom and physical suffering in the name of a grand idea. The theology of this tradition, i.e. the Judeo-Christian and Islamic theology of self-sacrifice, is hateful of democracy in the sense that Jacques Rancière writes of "the hatred of democracy." (Rancière 2006) It is hateful of the idea that everyone is equally competent enough to participate in the building of a just society. It is also hateful of the bodily, of individuality as linked to a mortal body, and its finality vis-à-vis the immortality of the great idea. Such structure of a world (in Larulle's sense, a universe of language, which is no less material or real, i.e. a universe determined by the real) is fundamentally religious, and more specifically, Abrahamic. Contrary to this, Marx's idea of commonality is profoundly individualistic, as the idea of equality is one materially established among the individuals in a society, rather than a detached, self-sufficient, or ubiquitous abstraction. As far as property is concerned, commonality should create a reality that is not only perceived, but also experienced – not only as collective, but also as individual – by each and every individual in a society.

The free associations of producers collectively hold possession of the means of production that originate in the commons of all products and forms of access to natural resources. The commons should effectively be equally and directly accessible to every-*body* in a society. The very logic of the structure of a community should determine the accessibility of the commons, as well as the collective or desired contributions to their creation, instead of coerced ones. It should be fundamentally democratic by way of enabling everyone to contribute equally to its re-production, and also by having unlimited access to the use of its products. The products are not commodities, as the surplus value is out of the equation. It is a radically different. At the dusk of capitalism, in the zone of the internet, communities appear that constitute commonality and produce common goods simultaneously. Their products are not final, they do not offer objects that can be manipulated, separated from the community, or commodified. Instead, they enable a process of continuous production. The mechanisms of control are set as internal rules of its productivity, determined in the last instance by a radically democratic concept of knowledge, which is one affected by the immanence of knowledge. The real of knowledge immanently affects the program of its production by allowing it to be constantly generated by the operations of knowledge as real or a matter in its own right, rather than by the philosophical agenda of a group of people who would programmatize the "development" of the community and its production. The mechanisms of control rely precisely on contradiction, conflicting knowledge or views, which are resolved in a way that is more a matter of craft than political power. Anonymity, in the sense of suspension of "auctoritas," is the mode of operation of the creative online communities. The anonymity at issue is not an effacement of the individual, but quite to the contrary, it results from the multitude of individuals that participate in it. The functioning of such a community and its production is fundamentally social, where the social is "superposed" (as in quantum theory) with the individual.

The analogy of superposition taken from Laruelle's non-standard philosophy (a term more often used in the latest stage of non-philosophy), and inspired by quantum theory, serves to enable us to understand the fundamentally social nature of the individual and its reverse, not as a paradox but as two realities that can be viewed unilaterally. The fact that they are viewed unilaterally does not mean that one does not affect the other as its real foregrounding and its determination in the last instance. As questions of temporality are not relevant for our discussion, we are neither interested in the issues of "simultaneity" of both realities, nor in the issues of "sequentiality." It is of no relevance to us whether the individual or the society comes first, neither in the temporal nor in the axiological sense. What matters is that the social constitutes a real in its own right, as does the human-in-human, and that one conditions the other by immanently affecting it.

Only in community does each individual have the means of cultivating his gifts in all directions; therefore, only in the community is personal freedom possible. In the previous substitutes for the community (e.g., in the State), personal freedom has existed only for the individuals of the bourgeois society, and only insofar as they were individuals of the ruling class, namely those who do not need to rely on their wage labor. (Karl Marx 1968)

The relations of the two realities ought to be regulated in a way that enables the wellbeing of the bodies that constitute the society as its communist determination in the last instance. Whether the individual engenders society, or the other way around, is a fundamentally philosophical question, one of assigning values in the axiological sense that boils down to theology. The question of the eventual "superposition" of the two realities, a method suggested by Laruelle in his project of non-standard philosophy borrowing from quantum theory, would not be a non-philosophical one, in spite of the intention. Exploring this issue in such manner would be a self-indulging, purely speculative, and an auto-referential project, as it is of no direct relevance for the social praxis that is subject to our study. It is inoperative with regard to the project of creating a society that enables equality and wellbeing for every-body, and is therefore irrelevant for the subject matter of this study. Methodological questions in sciences are determined by the subject matter (or "the material") of research. The subject matter in our case is "a transcendental material" that is in its last instance linguistic, namely the political, and is determined by a real that has its own intrinsic laws. It may be an abstraction, but it is a real abstraction (Sohn-Rethel 1978). It requires a language of universality. However, universality is not the same as generality. The concept of superposition borrowed directly from quantum theory operates as a generalization, as it is not the product of a radicalization of a singular and unilaterally postulated real.

Prof. Dr. Katerina Kolozova, Institute in Social Sciences and Humanities - Skopje,
katerina.kolozova[at]isshs.edu.mk

References

Financial Crisis Inquiry Commission (FCIC). *The Financial Crisis Inquiry Report: Final Report of the National Commission on the Causes of the Financial and Economic Crisis in the United States*. Washington, DC: U.S. Government Publishing Office, 2011.
Kolozova, Katerina. *The Cut of the Real: Subjectivity in Poststructuralist Philosophy*. New York: Columbia University Press, 2014.
Kolozova, Katerina. *Towards a Radical Metaphysics of Socialism: Marx and Laruelle*. Brroklin, New York: punctum books, 2015.

Marx, Karl. *Capital: A Critique of Political Economy, Vol. 3: The Process of Capitalist Production: Interest and Profit of Enterprise*, ed. Frederick Engels. New York: International Publishers, 1894. Web. <http://www.marxists.org/archive/marx/works/1894-c3/ch23.htm>

Marx, Karl. *Economic and Philosophical Manuscripts 1844.* Moscow: Progress Publishers, 1959a. Web. <http://www.marxists.org/archive/marx/works/1844/manuscripts/wages.htm>.

Marx, Karl. "Third Manuscript: Private Property and Communism," in idem. *Economic and Philosophical Manuscripts of 1844.* Moscow: Progress Publishers, 1959b. Web. <https://www.marxists.org/archive/marx/works/1844/manuscripts/comm.htm>.

Marx, Karl. "Feuerbach: Opposition of the Materialist and Idealist Outlooks," in idem. *The German Ideology.* Moscow: Progress Publishers, 1968. Web. <https://www.marxists.org/archive/marx/works/1845/german-ideology/ch01.htm>.

Laruelle, François. *Philosophie et non-philosophie.* Liege: Pierre Mardaga, 1989.

Laruelle, François. *Introduction au non-marxisme.* Presses Universitaires de France: Paris, 2000.

Laruelle, François. *From Decision to Heresy: Experiments in Non-Standard Thought.* New York: Urbanomic x Sequence Press, 2012.

Rancière, Jacques. *Hatred of Democracy.* London: Verso, 2006.

Rancière, Jacques. "Time, Narrative, and Politics," *Identities: Journal for Politics, Gender and Culture,* 11.1 (2014): 7-18.

Sohn-Rethel, Alfred. *Intellectual and Manual Labor: Critique of Epistemology.* London: Macmillan, 1978.

Williams, Alex and Nick Srnicek. "#Accelerate: Manifesto for an Accelerationist Politics," *Critical Legal Thinking,* May 14, 2013. Web. <http://criticallegalthinking.com/2013/05/14/accelerate-manifesto-for-an-accelerationist-politics >.

ADAM LOUIS KLEIN (New York)

Peace between Trotskyism and Maoism: Non-Maoism and Double Superposition

Abstract

Non-Philosophy is a rigorous practice that can have useful applications for academic researchers and political activists alike. Utilizing its methods and frameworks, it is possible to bring Peace into the endless War of sectarian tendencies in which "the Left" is mired. In the following paper, we apply the technique of Non-Philosophy to Josh Moufawad-Paul's pamphlet "Maoism or Trotskyism," taking it as an instance of occasional material to be transformed. An important aspect of this analysis is a syntactical deployment of Non-Philosophy not always found in non-philosophical texts: here our dualysis proceeds by *double* (and not only single) superposition. We effectuate *two* non-philosophical clones, using the first in order to recursively effectuate a second. First, we transform Trotskyism by isolating its philosophical and auto-positional structure, then we use this radicalized Trotskyism in order to transform Moufawad-Paul's Maoist polemic. The result is a radicalized Maoism-Trotskyism opening the way towards a productive and integrative Peace between Trotskyism and Maoism.

Keywords: François Laruelle, J. Moufawad-Paul, Non-Philosophy, Maoism, Trotskyism, Marxism

Non-Philosophy in-Struggle

Today capitalism is manifesting once again its fundamentally crisis-ridden and thwarted nature. The Crisis cuts the social body and the specters of fascism (not always so spectral) reemerge. Where is the so-called Left, the authentically politicized Left that might herald what Alain Badiou has called "The Idea of Communism," posing it as a real and effective alternative to auto-poetic Capital, relentlessly absorbing the social in both intension and extension? It is often remarked that the specifically and explicitly Marxist or Communist Left has been in shambles for a long time, mired in sectarian squabbles and near-irrelevancy. Might there be an *immanent reason* for this, and could not we locate this reason, not exactly to "transcend" it, but to radicalize its own resources? Indeed, the thinking of Non-Philosophy allows us to isolate *the dogmatic and aporetic structure* that underlies sectarianism, and to transform such a structure into an integrative Peace between tendencies, a Peace in-struggle.

In this text, we will isolate such an aporetic and philosophical structure at play in the conflict between Maoism and Trotskyism. We will see how the *polemical form*, here exhibited in Josh Moufawad-Paul's Maoist polemic "Maoism or Trotskyism"[1] articulates an unsolvable circularity that must be transformed if we are to radicalize communist theory and practice. The productive and integrative Peace between Trotskyism and Maoism that emerges will find its concrete image in the figure of the united front.

When bringing together Maoism and Trotskyism, it is true that we cannot deny the deep sectarianism, orthodoxy, and conformism that runs through much of present day Trotskyism, especially in the Anglophone world. In fact, taking up a 'politics of the Real' might already seem to privilege Maoism, and yet a non-philosophical treatment demands that we renounce any transcendent access: any birds-eye view of the two tendencies whereby we might perform a mediating synthesis. We must at all costs avoid a banal, "centrist" Marxism, or even an unrigorous eclecticism. It is necessary to approach Maoism and Trotskyism from a *single side*, that is, uni-versally. This is the side of the foreclosed Real, which allows us to subtract from the conflictual and hierarchical duality of "Trotskyism vs. Maoism." There is no meta-language, in politics especially; nor is there a "balance" between Maoism and Trotskyism. If anything, their only common core is what throws them both into a certain *imbalance*.

Yet such an imbalance can and will show itself to be a productive and integrative discordance, since irreducible to philosophical War: the war of opinions, positions, dogmas, and polemics. It is an imbalance that arises from allowing the Real to be given-without-givenness. In order to achieve such a discordant harmony requires here that we know how to handle the precise, formal operations of the non-philosophical technique that we shall employ. First, however, we must elucidate what we mean by the aporetic structure of the polemic.

Polemic as Aporia and War

Moufawad-Paul's text "Maosim or Trotskyism" is not a vulgar text. As he assures us, "to ask the question 'Maosim or Trotskyism' as a Maoist is to try to investigate Trotsky-

---

[1] The polemic features as an appendix to Josh Moufawad-Paul's *Continuity and Rupture: Philosophy In The Maoist Terrain* (2016).

ism as a competing ideological current and to perform this investigation not to make sectarian points because of some religious adherence to the signifier 'Maoist' but in order to point out why Maoism rather than Trotskyism is a necessary theoretical rallying point if we want to make revolution" (Moufawad-Paul 2016, 230). For Moufawad-Paul, the question is to determine whether or not Maoism or Trotskyism is better suited as a theory and practice of revolution that has learned from the past and is relevant to the present and future. The real problem is ultimately that Trotskyism is a "theoretical tradition that has so far proven itself incapable of being a revolutionary science" (Moufawad-Paul 2016, 231). This is because, quite simply, Trotskyism is a "dead-end" having shown itself incapable of making revolution, the very *point* of communist politics (Moufawad-Paul 2016, 233). This incapacity, Moufawad-Paul thinks, can be located in the basic Trotskyist theory of Permanent Revolution.

One cannot help but be impressed by Moufawad-Paul's desire to engage the problem from the standpoint of a genuine, ideological line struggle that aims to clarify and strengthen political practice. On top of this, his arguments are persuasive and illuminating. He at least seems to show that within the Trotskyist theory of permanent revolution "there is a tension here between the desire to break away from dogmatic applications of historical materialism and the gut reaction to stay within the safe territory of a "pure" Marxism" (Moufawad-Paul 2016, 237). That is, there are indeed *theoretical* reasons that might help us understand contemporary Trotskyist Conformism. However, there are at least several moments in the essay when one cannot help but think a kind of strawman of Trotskyism is emerging, in particular when Moufawad-Paul argues that Trotskyists "examine the failure of the Soviet Union as the result of an evil individual who possessed the power to produce a bureaucracy devoted to his nefarious plans (the kind of analysis that belongs in fairy tales and fantasy fiction), [while] Maoists try to make sense of the failures of the Soviet Union in a historical-materialist manner" (Moufawad-Paul 2016, 254). Surely, a consistent Trotskyist would give a *social* reason for this failure: the backward character of the productive forces, the material conditions.

But let us ask somewhat naively, yet with our non-philosophical goals in mind: how would a strawman *not* end up being produced here? Isn't it the character of these "debates," of these polemics that strive to give a kind of "proof" of their position, demolishing the other side once and for all, that there will always be a last vestige, a last refuge from where to cry "strawman!"? Indeed, we can even notice, empirically, the proliferation of polemics that arose in order to counter Moufawad-Paul[2], and even if we find Moufawad-Paul's "more convincing," do we not see here a kind of ever-present possibility, that of an endless *back-and-forth*?

Non-Philosophy identifies the structure of Philosophy as possessing something like this "back-and-forth" movement of the polemic. A more formal definition of Philosophy will be given below, but suffice it to say that Philosophy encompasses polemic due to three of its features: arbitrariness, auto-position, and totalization.

The arbitrariness of Philosophy indicates the necessity for a "first premise" (which is different from an axiom in the non-philosophical sense), which can also mean the initial *field of operation* that Philosophy takes. Auto-position is correlative to arbitrariness, meaning that it is none other than the position of Philosophy itself which 'Decides' to posit itself there – according to this or that premise, enacting its operations in this or that field. Lastly, totalization accounts for the attempt not only to operate according to a self-posited field, but to *reflectively over-determine* this field, limiting it, enclosing it and securing disclosure and determination according to its own terms.

Relative to polemic this means that, qua arbitrarily positing, the polemicist always "misses" another possible space of position, from which the opponent can then declare a strawman, and also reciprocally auto-position. As auto-position, polemic is incapable of extending towards this outside-space, to exist 'beyond' the original premise or field in which it has anchored itself. Lastly, as totalization, Polemic takes itself to be "demolishing," or once and for all invalidating the other side, though this can only result in a "transcendental appearance" given the relativity of its initial position. These three features collectively determine the philosophical, and thus polemical, structure as being *relative-absolute*, as Laruelle puts it. The arbitrariness of the posit taints Philosophy with inherent relativity, while its pretention to totalization and thus absoluteness gives it a dogmatic form. The "back-and-forth" movement is engendered by the space of "debate" that thus emerges: the possibility of continued auto-position from either side, due to the reproducibility of the aforementioned conditions. This is Polemic's status as War, as *polemos*. This War is aporetic: as long as auto-position is operative, there is no solution to the polemics that will wage "on both sides," and strawmen are constitutively possible, even inevitable.

---

[2] See Downing 2016 as well as Goldner 2012.

Formal Exposition of Non-Philosophical Technique

The wager here is that a non-philosophical treatment will allow us to transform, while simultaneously radicalizing, this War, this *polemos*, opening up the possibility of an integrative Peace-in-struggle. We will lay out the Non-Philosophical operations we will employ first of all in a formal manner.

There are three moments to be identified in a non-philosophical process (a dualysis):

1) An axiomatic (non-)positing of the Real. We call this a (non-)positing because it does not start from an "intuitively" given premise. It is stated in an *axiomatic* way, using terms drawn from occasionally provided materials, defined implicitly by their operation. This allows the (non-)posit to act as neutralizing *bracket* or *epoché*, allowing the Real to be *given* (without a horizon of givenness) and undermining Philosophical pretensions. The Real is The One. It is *immanent-(to-)itself*.

2) Philosophical Invariant. The Philosophical Invariant is the auto-positional structure of those practices and discourses that must be transformed by Non-Philosophy. It is a structure based on foundational Decisions that split the Real-One and proceed to mediate and over-determine this split (a 2/3 or 3/2 configuration). The axiomatic (non-)positing of the Real underdetermines the pretensions of such foundational Decisions (1). Such an auto-positional structure can receive other 'names'[3]: Philosophy, but also World, Capital, Conformism, or Orthodoxy, etc. In this text, we add Polemic.

3) The clone of Philosophy (or of World, Capital, Conformism, etc.). The clone is Non-Philosophy, this thinking itself. It requires materials provided by those practices and discourses that come ready-made in their auto-positional structure (2). Through an axiomatic (non-)positing of the Real (1) the structure of these materials are depotentialized and are opened up for a usage which is in accordance with the Real, or in immanent identity. The practice of Non-Philosophy is simultaneously the isolation and identification of the philosophical invariant (2) and its transformation through the axiomatically (non-) posited given that is the Real (3).

---

[3] The discursive 'stuff' of Non-Philosophy consists of a repository of such names. These involve the names used in the axiomatic statements that (non-)posit the Real, the names which indicate the philosophical invariant, and also the "non" that signals the cloning operation. The relation between such names is an order-relation and non-commutative *syntax* – not graphically, but with respect to conceptual function.

Though we have three moments, Non-Philosophy is a procedure of *dual-ysis*, not a 3/2 structure of dialectical mediation like Philosophy. The outcome of Non-Philosophy consists only of the Real and the clone, which is simply the material first received in auto-positional form, as transformed by the Real. The dual structure is in-One, as the clone is only a relative autonomy determined-in-the-last-instance by the radical autonomy of the Real-One. It is a unilateral duality *without mediation or transcendent synthesis*.

A Case Requiring Double Superposition

How might this method be applied to the Trotskyist-Maoist War? We must analyze a given discourse as material, locate its philosophical structure, and construct from it a clone that will be determined-in-the-last-instance by the Real. Here we are dealing with two discourses as material – Maosim and Trotskyism - and we wish set them into play. For this reason, this text will attempt to engage a non-philosophical process not always found in the existing works of Non-Philosophy –we will produce *two clones* and set these clones in relation to each other.

In order for us to avoid all transcendent mediation and synthesis – any kind of 'Marxist centrism' or eclectic Compromise– we must make sure that we do not leave the confines of dualysis. We cannot take two clones and synthesize them by a third term. The key here will be to employ a recursive process that is uni-versal all the way down. Laruelle often represents the cloning operation as a kind of $1+1=1$[4]. The clone is added to the Real, but the Real remains unaltered, in immanence and in-One: so the result remains 1. If the idea of $1+1=1$ accounts for a single cloning process, we could say that a recursive use of clones conforms to the idea of $1+1+1=1$. We are dealing with something like an idempotent operation recursively applied to its own results. We arrive at a superpositional fusion of the two clones – let's call it Maosim-Trotskyism. Such is an operation of double superposition.

Concretely, the strategy we will follow is to first clone Trotskyist discourse, taking as our material Leon Trotsky's work *The Permanent Revolution*. Our Trotskyist clone will be an Internationalism thwarted by a 'peasant' Real. Then, we will superpose this radicalized Trotskyist clone upon J. Moufawad-Paul's Maoist polemic. The result will be a complex theoretico-discursive object manifesting the atonal unity of a united front.

---

[4] As one example, see Laruelle 2012.

Non-Trotskyism as Internationalist Clone

Axiomatic (non-)positing of the Real – Revolutionary Internationalism.
Philosophical Invariant – The Theory of the Permanent Revolution forms an autopositional doublet in relation to The Theory of Socialism In One Country, or "Stalinism."
Transcendental science-pragmatics – Non-Trotskyism as Internationalist clone.

Here our non-philosophical treatment in a certain sense runs parallel with what Moufawad-Paul has accomplished in his polemic, if only in so far as to locate the tendency to Trotskyist conformism in the nature of the theory of Permanent Revolution. Where it differs is a theoretical treatment whose own form is irreducible to Conformism as such, that is, a form that has subtracted itself from the endless back-and-forth of the strawman. Indeed, what is at issue in Trotskyism's Conformist structure is a doublet whereby the conflict between Trotskyism and "Stalinism" is elevated to a universal position, indeed according to the terms of Trotskyism (3/2 structure). This is perhaps the real core of the monolithic usage of the term "Stalinism" of which Moufawad-Paul complains (Moufawad-Paul 2016, 241). As Trotsky writes, "the theory of socialism in one country, which rose on the yeast of the reaction against October, is the only theory that consistently and to the very end opposes the theory of the permanent revolution" (Leon Trotsky 1931, 143), and at the same time, "the theory of the permanent revolution now demands the greatest attention from every Marxist, for the course of the class and ideological struggle has fully and finally raised this question from the realm of reminiscences over old differences of opinion among Russian Marxists, and converted it into a question of *the character, the inner connections, and methods of the international revolution in general*" (Trotsky 1931, 143) (my emphasis). The doublet of Permanent Revolution and Socialism In One Country is indeed meant to envelop the conflict between communist revolution and its fidelity and counter-revolution understood on a global scale: "the struggle is between the basic ideas of Marx and Lenin on the one side and the eclecticism of the centrists on the other" (ibid., 145).

Indeed, this problem cannot be adequately confronted without understanding the complexities of *fidelity* to revolution, and much of Trotsky's *Permanent Revolution* involves a certain amount of quibbling as to whether or not he and Lenin had always been on the same page regarding the basic notions that the Permanent Revolution expresses, indeed, whether or not his theory his faithful to revolution and to "the basic ideas of Marx and Lenin." As is historically the case, it is the problematics of fidelity to revolutionary events that originally raises all the problems of splits and divergences within a movement. Following revolutionary change, the basic question becomes: how to move forward? To be fair, we could even see the dyad that envelops Trotsky's discourse as a question of preserving the *singularity* of a revolutionary event that places certain irreconcilable demands on how to bear forth its continuation, thus indeed requiring that "the question of program is in turn inseparable from the question of two *mutually exclusive theories*" (ibid.,145) (my emphasis).

We are thus dealing with a general problem of revolution: the almost necessary fact of splits due to the character of fidelity to a singular event. Even as these splits arise from the authentic desire to carry through such an event –without ceding or comprising on its revolutionary potential –the dyadic nature of the different branches of fidelity harbors the inherent possibility of an ossification into the 3/2 structure of a self-enclosed and Conformist auto-position, as each fidelity attempts to assert itself as the "one true way."

In a world decades after the fall of the Berlin Wall, but wherein the communist program once again must be revived and be put on the order of the day, the question is *how to retain yet reinvigorate* fidelities, such that they might "merge," intersect, and develop without compromise. To preserve this fidelity, let us *axiomatically (non-)posit the Real kernel of Trotskyism, i.e Internationalism.* The core of communist revolution and human emancipation is a worldwide movement: Revolution is Internationalist or it is nothing.

Yet, this internationalism as deployed in Trotsky's work seems to meet its limits in the "problem of the peasantry." It is notable that most of the debate between Trotsky and those grouped behind Stalin centers around the role of the peasantry, and it is this that continues to rage as the point of contention between Trotskyists and Maoists, in so far as Maoists accord a far greater revolutionary potential to the peasants under certain conditions. Here again we have a conflict between two fidelities, this time Maoism and Trotskyism, each in fact claiming a fidelity to Lenin/Marx. One might say whereas Trotsky aims to show his essential concordance with Lenin, Mao develops his theories as a concordance with Lenin that is modulated and transformed by the application to Chinese conditions. Mao*ism* then understands this application to have ultimately introduced new and universal elements into Marxism: what J. Moufawad-Paul calls a relationship of "continuity and rupture."[5] Is it not that the peasantry forms a kind of symptomal point in the discourse that surrounds the Trotskyist dyad of Permanent Revolution and Socialism In One Country? And is it not this point that allows Trotskyist discourse to operate a kind of exclusion whereby Maoism is invalidated – grouped in with "Stalinism" – *a priori*? Indeed, this is the core of the problem.

Interestingly, Trotsky maintains that in so far as Lenin came to side with him with respect to the question of the peasantry, still for Lenin the relationship of the proletariat and the peasantry "retained a somewhat algebraic character" (ibid., 141). The quantities and proportions of this relationship, as well as its party-political form, were left underdetermined. It is this determination and fixation of algebraic variables that Trotsky provides, ensuring us that he remains faithful to Lenin. The peasant must be definitively subordinated to proletarian leadership, for "no matter how great the revolutionary role of the peasantry may be, it nevertheless cannot be an independent role and even less a leading one" (Leon Trotsky 1931,1451). But is not this algebraic character of Lenin's position exactly the point where there is a *necessary* indeterminacy? In other words, we move in Trotsky from indeterminacy to determinacy. Is this not the moment where a Decision, or at least the possibility of the 3/2 auto-positional structure begins to constitute itself?

A non-philosophical treatment in fact holds itself at the level of this "algebra." It interprets the variables of a problematic 'one time, each time,' admitting that the Real can only ever be *modelled*. In this sense, (non-)positing the Real as Internationalism means that this Internationalism can never be prematurely closed by a too hasty auto-positional determination: a "transition from variables to constants" that would take itself to be more than a simple model which responds to a given conjuncture. Uni-versality, however, arises in this "infinite" possibility of modelization, in so far as "Internationalism" is only ever a "maxim." It is the Real upon which we cannot compromise, but which only *receives its name* from the given material (here, from Trotsky/ism).

Non-Trotskyism, we will say, is an Internationalism, faithful to Lenin, refusing to capitulate to class collaboration and "bureaucratic" degeneration, though always allowing itself to 'rest at' its algebraic character. This so even as at every moment we *must* determine, must act, must *model*, but it is only ever that.

---

[5] Per the title of his book *Continuity & Rupture: Philosophy In The Maoist Terrain*, in which "Maoism or Trotskyism" features as an appendix. The concept of "continuity and rupture" accounts for how "Marxist science" must retain fidelity to past events, while at the same time rupturing with outdated theories that must be updated according to practico-revolutionary experience.

It is exactly at this level that there is no contradiction with Maoism. Non-Trotskyism is of an "algebraic" nature, and the class compositions which model it in terms of a present political struggle remain to be "filled in." The process of this filling in and modeling is an experimental practice for which all the works of Trotsky and other Trotskyists can serve as tools.

Application of Double Superposition

Axiomatic (non-)positing of the Real – Cultural Revolution.

Philosophical Invariant – The Polemical Form as auto-positional, reintroducing Capital into the communist movement.

Transcendental science-pragmatics – Continuity-and-rupture-between-Maoism-and-Trotskyism as clone of J. Moufawad-Paul's Maoist polemic. Reinitiating of fidelity in a superposed manner, making use of Non-Trotskyism.

It is time to insert our Non-Trotskyist clone into the problematic of J. Moufawad-Paul's polemic, performing a double superposition. Of course, in the context of Moufawad-Paul's polemic, the polemical form ensures an infinitesimal receding of the strawman relative to Trotskyism. Indeed, Moufawad-Paul's goal is to disqualify Trotskyism, to exclude it once and for all from any hope of fidelity, from any genuine continuity and rupture, which accounts for the dynamics of authentic revolutionary fidelity. Is this discursive operation even possible relative to *Non*-Trotskyism?

It is evident that it is not. In the hands of Non-Trotskyism, The Theory of the Permanent Revolution is more like a set of "maxims" or "principles" which are modelled by Trotskyist materials in the always-conjunctural struggle against Stalinism. Wherever there is something like Stalinism, Non-Trotskyism has the means to intervene and be politically efficacious. Non-Trotskyism then acts as a basic kind of *resistance* to J. Moufawad-Paul's polemic, for it has side-stepped its very structure. Thus, our Non-Trotskyist clone becomes the starting point for a cloning operation upon Moufawad-Paul's text in a recursive manner.

Moufawad-Paul is intent on showing his reader that while Trotskyism is a "dead-end," Maoism is innovative, and that it has managed to build on past revolutionary experiences to develop new theories with a universal scope: this is part of its "continuity and rupture" (Moufawad-Paul 2016, 230). Of particular importance are the transformations in theory and practice developed in response to the experience of the Cultural Revolution. The experience of the Cultural Revolution changes communist practice in at least two ways: 1) we now know that class struggle continues under socialism, and in particular expresses itself at the ideological level 2) a "party of a new type"[6] requires that Cultural Revolution is in a sense there from the beginning, constituting part of a constant line struggle and ideological self-criticism to ensure commitment to the proletarian cause. Whereas according to Moufawad-Paul, Trotskyists attribute the failures of the Soviet Union to an evil individual with nefarious plans (a possible point of entry for a strawman), Maoists have a robust theory of possible degeneration that takes into account class struggle and the role of ideology.

If we take Maoism seriously, we can see to what degree Maoism at least harbors the possibility of admitting a political practice in itself capable of undoing auto-positional structures, in so far as it rests on constant ideological critique and the need to constantly reground itself in the Real of class struggle. Such in fact makes Maoism quite close in spirit to Non-Philosophy. And yet, this does not mean that Maoism has expunged itself of auto-positional circles, as is of course evidenced by Moufawad-Paul's polemic. Here, we attempt to purify and radicalize Maoism using the material that is Moufawad-Paul's polemic. Thus, we are enacting a certain kind of Non-Maoism. A more general non-philosophical treatment of Maoism is also possible.[7]

In order to understand how this will function, we have to understood in which way a homology between Capital and Philosophy is key to Non-Philosophy. The auto-positional structure is an *invariant*, a formal matrix, such that it allows homological identifications between different "contents." Philosophy and Capital are both auto-positional structures[8] and to this we may add, as already identified, Polemic, or the polemical form. It is in this sense that Moufawad-Paul's polemic falls short of the most radical aspirations of Maoism. It performs – in the very act of its discourse – exactly what Cultural Revolution aims to

---

[6] J. Moufawad-Paul asserts that Maoism was first formalized as such by the Revolutionary Internationalist Movement [RIM] in the late 1980's and early 1990's. What is there called a "party of a new type" is a party that would synthesize the lessons of the Cultural Revolution at every moment in its practice (see Revolutionary Internationalist Movement, 1993).

[7] See Klein 2017 for a preliminary development of Non-Maoism in general, taken up without reference to Trotskyism.

[8] To understand how Capital acts as auto-positional, we only need to consult Marx's magisterial explication of the functioning of Capital as "automatic subject" and "positing its own presuppositions" (Marx 1986).

guard against: it reproduces Capital within the communist movement itself, in the form of polemical auto-position.

It is indeed by continuity and rupture that a fidelity is woven to the Real while being able to continue and develop. If we see Non-Trotskyism as a fidelity *constitutively excluded* by the polemic of Moufawad-Paul, we see how such a fidelity – qua excluded – can provide us with the tools to underdetermine the auto-positional machine of the Polemic. The key to a non-philosophical treatment is always to "get outside of" Philosophy, and it is Non-Trotskyism that has provided us with this preliminary side-step.

Non-Trotskyism, as we have developed it, is an algebraic class composition whose maxim is the unavoidable need for proletarian Internationalism. It is a possible modeling of class alliances and tactics that persists in confronting and challenging Stalinism at any given conjuncture. Cultural revolution, on the other hand, demands constant line struggle and self-criticism to maintain the proletarian cause. There is no contradiction here.

This is the point where argument stops, at least in the philosophical sense. We allow the Real to be given-without-givenness, an *axiomatic* (non-)posit. Its name here is *Cultural Revolution*. The two – Non-Trotskyism and Maoism – can now fuse by the cloning of material. Moufawad-Paul's text acts as material from which a *continuity and rupture* results as clone: continuity entwined and entangled with rupture, subtending the relation between Maoism and Trotskyism as two fidelities. In other words, it is their very discordance which allows them to remain conjunctural possibilities of modelization oriented to concrete material, a material equally discordant and diffuse, which in fact demands non-harmonious – ruptural – solutions. At the same time, Maosim and Trotskyism can remain continuous in-One. We have "ensured" this via non-philosophical thinking. Continuity and rupture emerges thus as a clone of Moufawad-Paul's text, the non-philosophical Identity of Maoism and Trotskyism. This discordant, atonal, and undulatory fusion of Maoism and Trotskyism, tracing the complex paths of fidelity: let us call it Maoism-Trotskyism, the result of a double superposition.

Concrete Image of Maoism-Trotskyism

It would not be inappropriate for a non-philosophical treatment to end with an image, if only so as to ensure the materiality of its formalisms and theory, the sensibility of its thought, and its status as praxis. What we have attempted here to construct is nothing but a theoretical apparatus whose form might be modelled by the practice of a *united front*.⁹ This intersection of theory and practice, axioms and model, syntax and semantics, is a relationship that future non-philosophical (and non-political) experimentation could explore. Ultimately, Maoism-Trotskyism does not demand that unity appear, nor does it demand that concrete Trotskyists and Maoists "accept" its argument (it is not exactly one). If anything, it is conjunctural; an experimentation in concrete circumstances, an attempt to think in a manner and according to a technique in which humans themselves might find use: in order to struggle, at last, in Peace.

Adam Louis Klein, The New School For Social Research, New York,
Department of Philosophy, adamlouisklein[at]gmail.com

References

Klein, Adam Louis. "Outline of Non-Maoism." 2017. Web. <http://www.adamlouisklein.com/thought/2017/10/29/outline-of-non-maoism>.

Downing, Gerry. "In Defense of Revolutionary Socialism, i.e. Trotskyism." *Socialist Fight*, 29 Aug. 2016. Web. <http://www.socialistfight.com/2016/08/26/in-defence-of-revolutionary-socialism-i-e-trotskyism>.

Goldner, Loren. "Notes Towards A Critique of Maoism," *Insurgent Notes: Journal of Communist Theory and Practice*, Oct.15, 2012. Web. <http://www.insurgentnotes.com/2012/10/notes-towards-a-critique-of-maoism>.

Marx, Karl. *Capital Vol. 1*. London: Penguin Books, 1986.

Moufawad-Paul, Josh. *Continuity and Rupture: Philosophy in the Maoist Terrain*. Croydon: Zero Books, 2016.

Mullarkey, John, and Anthony Paul Smith. *Laruelle and Non-Philosophy*. Edinburgh: Edinburgh University Press, 2012.

---

⁹ For a detailed discussion of the manner in which a theoretical apparatus or "theoretical installation" might take an empirical object or structure as model for its construction, see Laruelle's *Photo-Fiction: A Non-Standard Apparatus* (Laruelle 2012), in which a non-philosophical matrix is construed as a philosophico-photographic apparatus using the physical camera as a model.

Laruelle, François. "Non-Philosophy, Weapon of Last Defense: An Interview with François Laruelle," in Smith, Anthony Paul, and John Mullarkey (eds.). Laruelle and Non-Philosophy. Edinburgh, UK: Edinburgh University Press, 2012a. 238-251.

Laruelle, François, and Drew Burk. *Photo-Fiction, A Non-Standard Aesthetics*. Minneapolis: 2012b.

Revolutionary Internationalist Movement [RIM]. "Long Live Marxism-Leninism-Maoism!", *BannedThought.net: Struggling Against the Suppression of Ideas*, 26 December 1993. Web. <http://www.bannedthought.net/International/RIM/AWTW/1995-20/ll_mlm_20_eng.htm>

Trotsky, Leon. *The Permanent Revolution*. 1931. Scotts Valley: CreateSpace Independent Publishing Platform, 2014.

NICHOLAS EPPERT (New York)

(Black) Non-Analysis:
From the Restrained Unconscious to the Generalized Unconscious

Abstract

This paper is a contribution to the ongoing studies revolving around the fields of Afro-Pessimism and Non-Philosophy. It is focused mostly on a short essay that Francois Laruelle wrote in 1989 called "The Concept of Generalized Analysis or 'Non-Analysis" that eventually became part of a larger work called Theorie des Etrangers, *while also drawing on the latter for support. The focus is set not in terms of exegesis or commentary but in tandem with the work of Frank Wilderson III to borrow from both of their works and formulate a move from the "White restrained Unconscious" to the "(Black) generalized Unconscious". In the first section I articulate Laruelle and Wilderson's critiques of the common-sense image of the Unconscious. And in the second section I make the move from the White restrained Unconscious to the (Black) generalized Unconscious by arguing that the former is embedded within a metaphysical sovereignty of desires that excludes (Black) desires. The "White restrained Unconscious" is constituted by what Laruelle calls a "half loss" or a loss which loses itself. For this reason the (Black) generalized Unconscious cannot appear within it, for it is an absolute loss, or what Laruelle calls the Joui-sans-Jouissance. The White generalized Unconsicous blocks (Black) loss out by a transference mechanism. The opening up of the White restrained Unconscious to the (Black) generalized Unconscious which is its Identity in the last instance can only be done by "ending the World". Using Jared Sexton's notion of the "social life of social death" I show that this desire to end the world allows for a seeing from perspective of the "One" which is the subject position of the (Black) Non-Analyst and allows for a dualysis of the desires of the White restrained Unconscious.*

Keywords: Laruelle, afro-pessimism, (black) non-analysis, generalized unconscious, loss

The Critique of the Restrained Unconscious in Laruelle and Wilderson III

> *"What is missing in African-American cultural analysis is a concept of the 'one'"* Hortense Spillers (Spillers 1997, 140)

So imagine the following scenario: a white analysand is free-associating on the word 'black' before his black analyst. He is embarrassed because he can only think of negative words and mental associations; for some unknown reason, the word doesn't seem to conjure up any positive quality. Despite his attempts at repressing it, the word 'nigger' urges itself to the forefront of his mind, refusing to go away. He utters it, conscious of his own spiteful fury and with as much venom as he can muster-he has never, to his knowledge, used this word before. The analyst shows no response. Now even more embarrassingly conscious of his own stupid blind, and violently impotent rage, the anlysand thinks of another phrase: 'black nigger'. The association seems right; it seems to fit (despite himself), and what is more, it seems to mean something, but is not a phrase the analysand wants to utter here. He utters the word 'death' instead-a classic association, so banal in its obviousness, but reassuring nonetheless. The analyst nods with obvious enthusiasm and urges him to continue. (Marriott 2007, 223)

In a short essay entitled "The Concept of Generalized Analysis or 'Non-Analysis'," Francois Laruelle attempts to move from the conception of a "restrained Unconscious" to that of a "generalized Unconscious". The restrained Unconscious is defined by its invariant syntax of a Philosophical Decision of the unity of contraries of the One and the Dyad. It has "an amphibological appearance, the appearance of the identity or sameness of the Other. Between the *Other who is* (that of the Greco-metaphysical decision) and the *Other who 'is' not* (that of Judaism), there is an appearance of identity reduced to its most empirical forms or data". (Laruelle 1989, 508)[1] The Greco-metaphysical decision is a manifestation of Consciousness, or the "Self" whereas the "Other" represents the Judaic turn, representative of the Unconscious. In other words, the restrained Unconscious remains a firmly metaphysical or ontological entity. Where there should be One, Laruelle posits, this Philosophical Decision in the restrained Unconscious (consisting of the Greek Consciousness and the Judaic Unconscious) performs its philosophical division or rending in a "*resistance* (my italics) to the destruction of decision by an affect (of) the Other that risked being stronger than it" (Laruelle 1989, 508) Laruelle articulates an "enlarged or generalized concept of resistance," (Laruelle 1989, 513) which is the resistance that the restrained Unconscious or the everyday unconscious of the collective/individual *has to the One,* by hierarchizing one part of the Dyad, the Other of the Unconscious. This resistance is a resistance to the One, or the Stranger (to be discussed in the section on (Black) Non-Analysis).

Frank Wilderson III similarly provides a critique of the Unconscious that echoes the move from the restrained Unconscious to the generalized Unconscious in his book *Red,*

---

[1] All translations of Laruelle's "Le Concept d'Analyse Generalisée ou de 'Non-Analyse'" were made by consulting the original text as well as Taylor Adkin's translation on his blog. See Taylor Adkins, "Translation of Laruelle's 'The Concept of Generalized Analysis or of 'Non-Analysis," *Speculative Heresy*, June 15, 2013. Web. <https://speculativeheresy.wordpress.com/2013/06/15/translation-of-laruelles-the-concept-of-generalized-analysis-or-of-non-analysis/>.

Black and White: Cinema and the Structure of U.S. Antagonisms. Here, Wilderson makes a distinction between (White) Humans and (Blacks)[2] based on a fundamental antagonism. The violence done to (Blacks) is of the order of an ontological violence while, the violence done to those who are Human are merely "contingent conflicts" that Humans inflict on each other. They are "little family quarrels" of Whiteness.

> Rather, the gratuitous violence of the Black's first ontological instance, the Middle Passage, 'wiped out [his or her] metaphysics . . . his [or her] customs and sources on which they are based.' Jews went into Auschwitz and came out as Jews. Africans went into the ships and came out as Blacks. The former is a Human holocaust; the latter is a Human and a metaphysical holocaust. That is why it makes little sense to attempt analogy: the Jews have the Dead (the Muselmann) among them; the Dead have the Blacks among them. (Wilderson 2010, 38)

The very appearance of (Blacks) in the World is always-already an Anti-Black ontological violence or as Calvin Warren calls it "onticide," a "certain murderous operation through ontology." (Warren 2017, 407) since the being of the Slave is that of "social death" or the complete loss of kinship ties. Because of this metaphysical devastation there is thus a "ruse of analogy" between (Blacks) and Humans. As Wilderson argues, "No slave, no world. And in Addition, as Patterson argues, no slave is *in* the world. (Wilderson 2010, 11) (Blacks) cannot *appear* in the World. Humans have the privilege of metaphysical sovereignty and while violence can be done to a Jew, a Jew still has metaphysics, i.e. is still a White Human. The World, or ontology is constitutive of the erasure of (Blackness). This places the figure of the Slave as that by which the World parasites off of, and *enjoys* its metaphysical sovereignty. The Slave is the condition of the possibility of the World.

I would like to argue that Wilderson's ontological "ruse of analogy" carries over into the distinction between Laruelle's restrained Unconscious and the generalized. There is a ruse of analogy between the (Black) Unconscious and the White Unconscious. In his chapter on "The Narcissistic Slave" Wilderson still ascribes to a *restrained view of the Unconscious.* For Wilderson, the restrained Unconscious, synonymous with Lacanian analysis, is a (White) Human Unconscious in which (Black) speech is barred. For Wilderson, (Black-

---

[2] Here and throughout the rest of this paper, I adopt Anthony Paul Smith's grapheme of (Black) in parentheses that he utilizes in his book *Laruelle: A Stranger Thought* to indicate that (Blackness) does not appear within the World but is akin to Laruelle's Victim-in-Person. Of this grapheme, Smith says, "it relates fundamentally to the way, within the white world of philosophy the (Black) functions both as a blind spot, and as the structural negation of the human as philosophically overdetermined." (Smith 2016, 112)

ness) occupies the violently excluded Real of this Lacanian Unconscious. In this guise, Wilderson still subscribes to what Laruelle calls the restrained Unconscious, insofar as it is an Unconscious that is metaphysically sovereign, the only Unconscious that exists. However, a move to the generalized Unconscious asks what a (Black) desire "murdered" within ontology is like, and attempts to expand the Unconscious. It is important to make the distinction that the (restrained) *Unconscious as such is White* and *not* that White Humans have an Unconscious that is distinct from that of empirically black-skinned individuals. Everyone has a White Unconscious insofar as it is a restrained structure that partakes of the metaphysical sovereignty of the White Human. Indeed, as Frantz Fanon wrote of his Martinician compatriots, they underwent a "hallucinatory whitening (Fanon 2008, 80)" or an unconscious desire to be white. For Laruelle, this partakes of a Black/White Dyad that still belongs to the realm of metaphysical sovereignty or the philosophical decision. However, the ontological-psychoanalytic *resistance* that Laruelle argues that the restrained Unconscious has to the generalized Unconscious is synonymous with the resistance that a White Unconscious has to a (Black) Unconscious. This is a resistance to the One. While in restrained psychoanalysis, resistance is the defense of the ego to avow repressed memories or trauma, Laruelle's concept of a *generalized resistance* is a defense on the part of the White restrained Unconscious or the White Human to avow the trauma of what Laruelle calls the Stranger or the Victim-in-Person. This takes into account not only the individual's history, but the *lived history of the World*. Thus, Wilderson's ontological critique must be brought into his critique of the Unconscious. There is a ruse of analogy between the (Black) Unconscious and the White Unconscious.

I will therefore use the terms "White restrained Unconscious" and "(Black) generalized Unconscious" to denote Laruelle's movement from the restrained Unconscious to the generalized Unconscious in tandem with the necessity of the movement from a White Unconscious to a (Black) Unconscious. This move does not argue that all White Humans are *hiding* a (Black) Unconscious behind their White restrained Unconscious. It rather argues that the conception and science of the Unconscious hitherto formulated has been restrained by the structures of a White metaphysical sovereignty and can only articulate the restricted losses and desires of such a sovereignty. This is simultaneously a metaphysical and political critique. For Lacan, analysis consists of getting the analysand to become conscious of his or her relations with Others, synonymous to a kind of alienation. Wilderson's critique of metaphysics is simultaneously one of Civil Society that repeats itself in the Lacanian Symbolic.

The Other that Lacan speaks of, he says, are none other, "in the vernacular most salient to the Slave, Whites and their junior partners in civil society-Humans positioned by the Symbolic order" (Wilderson 2010, 70). The way Civil Society functions is via the metaphysical sovereignty of the White Human and the social death of the (Black) as outlined above. Further, the Symbolic order of the White restrained Unconscious functions similarly as constituting the desires of (Blackness) as socially dead or unable to appear.

Partly at issue here is that under the White restrained Unconscious the only subject that can have losses and desires are those that fall under the subject-positions of the Greek Conscious or the Judaic Other, or the Self/Other dynamic. While Laruelle uses the "Judaic turn" to denote a specific turn *within philosophy* that takes account of the Other, and not a racialization of philosophy, it is nevertheless the case that what counts as "Other" in this Judaic turn is a question of the Human, i.e. the one who has *metaphysics*. As Anthony Paul Smith notes, Laruelle's discussion of Judaic thought emphasizes how philosophers like Levinas and Derrida carry out a Judaic turn in philosophy and "their act of resistance to philosophy ends up as susceptible to capture and *colonization* (my italics) by philosophy." (Smith 2016, 99) For Wilderson, the White Other falls squarely within the policing of Philosophy and Civil Society and it ultimately fails by providing an inept structure of the Unconscious Other by *resisting* (Blackness) or the One. The Judaic Other provides a picture of mere contingent conflicts, mere family squabbles. Not only does the Unconscious come out as Conscious, and (White) Humans as Human, but (Blackness) comes out as White. The Unconscious is not deep enough, not dark enough. It is too White.

The metaphysical hierarchization between the Greek Consciousness and Judaic Unconscious must then cede to (Blackness) as a generalized Unconscious. The resistance that the restrained Unconscious has to the generalized Unconscious is a resistance of White Unconscious to (Blackness). For Laruelle, non-analysis, "is a way of taking up the problems of the world, of history, of philosophy, rather than those of simple consciousness as psychoanalysis does, but it is a way of taking them up which has some relationship with psychoanalysis." (Laruelle 2015a, 43) This is not to deny that there have been formulations of the White restrained Unconscious and psychoanalysis that take into account the collective unconscious, anthropology, and epiphylogenesis among other things. Rather to take account of the "problems of the world" in non-analysis is to take into account the desires and losses of those who do not *appear* within the confines of simple consciousness. Here, I endorse Anthony Paul Smith's articulation of the Stranger-Subject or Victim-in-Person as (Black) "to indicate that the identity is not given by the world, that this suspended identity is precisely closer to the Human-in-Human than the white human of philosophy. (Smith 2016, 116) Moving to the (Black) generalized Unconscious will allow for a "dualysis of restrained analysis" (Laruelle 1989, 514) in the or the White Unconscious in the Laruellian sense by transforming it into the material for analysis itself. This allows for an immanent (non)-analysis of the White restrained Unconscious by the (Black) generalized Unconscious. The (Black) generalized Unconscious functions by suspending the desires and objects of the White restrained Unconscious, and while not negating them, place them into reconsideration. (Blackness) or the "(subject) of science is the veritable 'analyst' in what we call 'non'-analysis'. This is an Unconscious without metaphysics, or a (Black) Non-Analysis.

Transference of Restrained Losses and the End of the World

There is a resistance of the White restrained Unconscious to the (Black) generalized Unconscious that is simultaneously a resistance to the One. What is this resistance and what does it entail? Wilderson argues that there is a "structural adjustment" or a move on the part of the Humans of Civil Society to force (Blackness) against its will to appear in the White restrained Unconscious as another member of Civil Society. In an interview conducted after the incidents in Ferguson, Missouri in 2014 and the shooting with Michael Brown, Wilderson says,

> Policing—policing Blackness—is what keeps everyone else sane. And if we can start to see the policing and the mutilation and the aggressivity towards Blackness not as a form of discrimination, but as being a form of psychic health and well-being for the rest of the world, then we can begin to reformulate the problem and begin to take a much more iconoclastic response to it. (Wilderson 2014, 7)

There is a way in which *repressing or resisting* (Blackness) allows one to keep one's sanity or mental health. This is because "normally people are not radical, normally people are not moving against the system: normally people are just trying to live, to have a bit of romance and to feed their kids." (Wilderson 2014, 9) Normal issues such as sanity, eating, loving, feeding kids, typical psychoanalytic issues, are ways of sublimating the fact of (Blackness), ways of policing (Blackness). These are ways of violently *forcing* (Blackness) to appear in the White restrained Unconscious. We can speak of this as another form of the ontological murder of (Blackness), except this time as the ontological murder of (Black) *desires*. Within the confines of normal desires, (Black) desires appear as always-already lost. As Jared Ball says, "it's almost like we need to reach out to find people around to the world to link up with. And then unfortunately we're let down when their anti-Blackness takes hold again (Wilderson 2014, 16)". The Others of Civil Society only partner up with (Blacks) until the "normal desires" of the former are attained and then Anti-Blackness as an attitude or a mode of "collective unconscious" takes hold again.

(Blackness) appears as the means by which desires in the White restrained Unconscious are able to take *object-form*. As Wilderson argues, "As an accumulated and fungible object, rather than an exploited and alienated subject, the Black is vulnerable to the whims of the world, and so is his or her cultural 'production'." (Wilderson 2010, 56) (Blackness) thus appears *alienated in the World* in the *object-form* that White desires take. These desires can desire *things that are lost in the World,* but they can never desire and take into account losses and desires are constitutively excluded from *appearing among the things of the World.* There is a difference of kind between (Black) desire and White desire. The latter appear as "normal desires" because they are *a priori* attainable or achievable in the "thought-world." They are thought to be attainable because they are desires *in the World.* As Wilderson reminds us, however, "No slave, no world. And in Addition, as Patterson argues, no slave is *in* the world. (Wilderson 2010, 11) This is a matter of desire that is intrinsic to the structure of the Unconscious. Wilderson notes this split subjectivity within himself when he says "But my huge weight fluctuation doesn't mean that when I'm thin and sick, that the world has gotten better for me as a Black person. I have to keep reminding myself that I am struggling for something for which there is no coherent articulation (Wilderson 2014, 16-17)". While the things of the World may appear as desires for Wilderson, they are but sublimated desires, repressed desires enacting an ontological ruse of analogy between normal desires and (Black) desires. This ruse is between desires that are within and outside the World.

This split subjectivity reveals itself in the utter ineptitude of the concept of loss in the White restrained Unconscious. Losses are typically imagined in terms of objects (in the World) whether imagined or real. If you imagine food as possible outcome of your actions it is not necessarily the case that you will receive it, and you will experience it as a present loss. Moreover, if you are given food, you will experience the possible future attainability or non-attainability as loss. This twofold structure of givenness and possibility is emblematic of the White restrained Unconscious and the Philosophical Decision. It is for this reason that Laruelle argues that the "normal desires" that Wilderson claims are part of a collective "libidinal economy" that gravitate around anti-Blackness partake of a "loss that a first time belongs to the structure and defines itself by the order of the signifier, then realizes itself a second time in the phantasmatic and imaginary modes, straight from the real." (Laruelle 1995, 281) For Laruelle, the restrained Unconscious is constituted by a twofold loss which is constitutive of metaphysics itself or the dynamic of the Greek Self and Judaic Other. The White restrained Unconscious because is always defined by a twofold loss. This is to say that the White restrained Unconscious desires things that always *lost twice*, and so these things are *never fully attainable*. If only given, the possible is always a loss, and if only possible, the given is always a loss. This double loss is a loss that *loses itself* within the Greco-Judaic structure. The White restrained Unconscious is not in fact determined by *loss as such, the loss of the World* but by the loss of *particular things* within the World. This inept concept of loss structures the White restrained Unconscious and so "restrained analysis conceals the unbearable quality of absolute loss (Laruelle 1989, 516)". No wonder that (Black) desires cannot appear within the White restrained Unconscious since what Laruelle is arguing in tandem with Wilderson is that *loss* does not belong to the White restrained Unconscious. The White restrained Unconscious has no *identity because it constantly loses itself in things* or what it calls its normal desires. Normal desires are but an inept concept of loss.

However, what defines the (Black) generalized Unconscious is a different kind of loss that functions by a unilateral duality that allows one to see the double losses of the White restrained Unconscious as determined in the last instance by an immanent loss. If (Blackness) is always already defined by loss within the framework of ontology, then the Unconscious of (Blackness) which is (Blackness) outside the confines of ontology would be, as David Marriott puts it in his book *Haunted Life,* the need to deal with the "loss of loss". In short the (Black) generalized Unconscious appears as lost within metaphysical sovereignty because the White restrained Unconscious forces the former to *lose itself.* It acts through the notion of of transference or the "bending-back [of] the unilaterality (of) the Unconscious through an imaginary identification that is also a denial of the subject (of) science." (Laruelle 1989, 516) The subject of science here is the (Black) analyst. Denying the "loss of a loss" the White restrained Unconscious attempts to project onto the (Black) generalized Unconscious a loss that loses itself, wherein the (Black) generalized Unconscious can no longer *identify itself.* The White restrained Unconscious refuses to take the analyst's desires into consideration and instead "bends-back" the strict unilaterality of the Victim-in-Person in order to project its Imaginary desires onto the analyst. As Laruelle says of the Victim-in-Person in *General Theory of Vic-*

tims, "the victim is twice victim, once as wronged in a criminal act, and a second time by effacement, albeit legally of the injury that had been suffered, an effacement whose publicity offends the victim (Laruelle 2015b, 64)". The ontological murder of (Blackness) is the first victimization by ontology and the second is the *misrepresentation of the victim*, the effacement of his desires by those who represent him. Transference thus acts as a re-iteration of the primal scene of ontological victimization, a repetition compulsion. The (Black) analyst here must teach the White analysand to overcome this repetition-compulsion.

The White restrained Unconscious must overcome this repetition-compulsion in order to acknowledge the desires of the (Black) generalized Unconscious. To see this another way Laruelle says that "[Restrained] analysis can only go as far as a *half-loss*, only going up to the mid-reunion.[3] (Laruelle 1995, 202) And it is this half-loss that is the transference of White desires onto the (Black) generalized Unconscious. It is the White restrained Unconscious telling the latter that all its losses and desires fall under the category of "normal desires". From this perspective there are no (Black) desires. It is not the case of these double losses that they are so absolute. Rather they are double, because they can never be attained and the loss loses itself all over again. They can never be attained because the loss is not immanent, it is not *lost enough*. The White restrained Unconscious has not lost enough. (Black) loss does not appear in the concept of White loss for the very reason that the latter does not exist. White loss only keeps losing itself. (Black) loss is already murdered within the metaphysical dictates of the Greek Self and Judaic Other of the White restrained Unconscious. There is then a ruse of analogy or philosophical decision made between the losses of the White restrained Unconscious and the (Black) generalized Unconscious. There is a "structural adjustment" that functions by making the "loss of loss" appear like "half-losses". The latter represses the former, which would be the end of the World as ontological field. As Laruelle argues, "The World is the Authority of Authorities, whereas the One defines the order of Minorities or Strangers." (Laruelle 2013, 168) The World is the authority on desires, creating the realm of normal desires between the Self and Other. Similarly, because the desires of the White restrained Unconscious take place *in the World,* these normal desires *pathologize* absolute loss as too radical, too (Black), too much a movement to a loss that is One. But a (Black) non-analysis attempts to put an end to the plane of half-loss itself, by "trying to destroy the world." (Wilderson 2014, 20) This is an attempt to destroy the World as the plane of realizability on which desires can occur. Daniel Colucciello Barber argues that the world is also given twice, the

---

[3] All translations of Laruelle's *Theorie des Etrangers* are my own.

"world-as-given *and* the world-as-possible," (Barber 183) and that the essential structure of analogy is this given twiceness. Connecting these themes to post-secularism and Afro-Pessimism, he argues that the World would then be the ruse of analogy, or the very ruse of ontological appearance. I would like to further add that the World is a ruse of the White restrained Unconscious. The World is the plane on which the double losses of the White restrained Unconscious occur. The question of the (Black) generalized Unconscious would be that of withdrawing libidinal investment in the World and the normal desires that adhere to it always-already murder (Black) desires. The opening up of the White restrained Unconscious to the (Black) generalized Unconscious would be the desire to end the World.

(Black) Non-Analysis

The movement to the (Black) generalized Unconsicous proceeds from the recognition of the desire to end the World. The end of the World opens up the way to the generalized Unconscious and the conception of an absolute loss. Laruelle identifies the position of the generalized Unconscious in the following way:

> The generalized Unconscious is the affect (of) loss, the a priori but immanent phenomenon (of) a loss without object. Loss lived as such by the subject rather than a loss affecting a subject. And if loss is an absolute and positive affect where "nothing", neither object nor world, neither being nor Being is lost, it signifies that there is nothing to retrieve or make return. There is a jouissance itself (of) loss, a non-thetic jouissance of the Unconscious where all is suspended without having to return and is thus lived in an immanent way in conformity with what is specific to man's essence. (Laruelle 1989, 518)

This is very similar to what Jared Sexton outlines as the "social life of social death":

> [Afro-pessimism] is a willing or willingness, in other words, to pay whatever social costs accrue to being black, to inhabiting blackness, to living a black social life under the shadow of social death…The affirmation of blackness, which is to say an affirmation of pathological being is a refusal to distance oneself from blackness in a valorization of minor differences that bring one closer to health, to life, or to sociality. (Sexton 2011, 27)

For Laruelle, the generalized Unconscious is constituted by an absolute loss. But this absolute loss, because it is absolute, must itself be lived in joy. This loss never loses itself. It never loses itself in a need to be re-found elsewhere in the White restrained Unconscious.

It never needs to be re-found, re-attained, re-achieved. And because it never loses itself, it is lived as immanent Identity. As Katerina Kolozova argues, "In non-philosophy, enjoyment and suffering no longer establish opposition. They are both instances of the lived, of the sheer experience that takes place as 'suffering'...One is subjected to a sensation, be it pleasure or pain, which place in the defenseless body through the instance of pure exposure or vulnerability (Kolozova 96)". This what in *Theorie des Etrangers* Laruelle calls Joui-sans-Jouissance, or the simultaneous lived experience of joy and pain without having to search for a jouissance that loses itself in an object. He says, "Joui is a stranger to the philosophical Ego, to the subject as "individual", always already divided, mixed eventually by jouissance in its philosophico-analytic concept (Laruelle 1995, 222)". Jouissance here denotes for Laruelle a divided enjoyment, one that was outlined by the concept of the double loss, an enjoyment that is always attenuated by a further loss. Joui, however, is without object. Similarly, Sexton argues that

> Fanon says that he wants to liberate the black man from himself, not repair his self-esteem or correct his misguided worldview or reacquaint him with some traditional way of life—not to heal him, but to liberate him. And liberation does not mean (only) to return the fruits of his formerly exploited labor or (only) to return the sovereignty of his people over their formerly colonized land or (only) to return control over the uses of his formerly enslaved body. Those are the external conditions, as it were. He must (also) be liberated from himself, from his self, from his desiring self. (Sexton 2017)

Because (Blackness) is already alienated and murdered in the World, to liberate the (Black) man from himself is not to return or re-find any *external object* of loss, but rather to destroy the field onto which (Blackness) ends up being projected, so that (Blackness) can enjoy itself as Joui-sans-Jouissance. The move to the (Black) generalized Unconscious is thus a conception of identification with itself in the last instance and a liberation of the (Black) man from himself. What Laruelle calls the Joui-sans-Jouissance is an immanent loss and affirmation, the experience of the (Black) self as such beyond historical and ontological transcendence, but nevertheless taking these transcendences into account, whether through the Middle Passage, on the auction block, or during the recent shootings in Ferguson, Missouri. As Sexton further argues, "separation, as psychoanalysis has shown powerfully, is a precondition for any relationship whatsoever." (Sexton 2017) The (Black) generalized Unconscious is not constituted by any *particular* losses, desires, or separations. What constitutes the (Black) generalized Unconscious is not separation or loss of the mother, of a native land, of property, or of any external factors. It is constituted by ontological loss or the very fact of loss and separation in and of themselves, the fact of social death and slavery. As such, the willingness to pay *whatever, any and all, past and future* social costs there are to being (Black) and affirming them is perhaps the necessity of formulating a (Black) generalized Unconscious. Moreover, if it is loss and separation themselves that belong to the (Black) generalized Unconscious, then there is an absolute jouissance of loss. Because this loss can never be realized in an object, there is nothing to regain. What belongs to the (Black) generalized Unconscious is immanent Identity itself. Such an immanent Identity is the domain of *freedom*. This Identity and desire is a separation from all transcendence, especially the World, since (Blackness) has never belonged to the World.

The subject of this immanent identity and this beginning point of freedom can be thought of as the (Black) non-analyst. Why the (Black) non-analyst? Laruelle says, "The subject (of) science is the veritable "analyst" in what we will call "non-analysis", and there is only a non-analyst who identifies itself with this subject and its immanent posture." (Laruelle 1989, 516) There is no analytic scene of analyst and analysand in Laruelle's non-analysis. However, the (Black) non-analyst here is the immanent identity of the White restrained Unconscious. It is the (Black) non-analyst to whom loss belongs to as Identity. The former sees from the perspective of the *Vision-in-One*. The "end of the World" as outlined by Afro-Pessimism can be thought of as the means by which the (Black) non-analyst works on the transcendental material of the White restrained Unconscious from the perspective of *the Vision-in-One*. It works on the desires of the White restrained Unconscious as an analyst works on the desires of an analysand, changing them morphing them, so that the latter can see from the perspective of the One. The end of the world denotes the end of metaphysical sovereignty and the identification in the last instance of the (Black) generalized Unconscious and the White restrained Unconscious. In Laruelle's *Theorie des Etrangers* he argues that Stranger is a "Self that is neither subjective nor objective, but immanent (to) itself, so that it is no longer divided between Self and Other, this one being no longer interior or exterior *and* exterior to the Self, but the Self exists immanently also itself, without "leaving" itself in a new structure which is that of the Stranger-it exists-Stranger." (Laruelle 1995, 13) This Stranger-Self can be used to describe the (non)-position of the (Black) generalized Unconscious. It is neither subjective, nor objective, partaking of neither Self nor Other, but radically constitutive of the Self/Other dynamic. Laruelle argues that this consists of an "ego-xeno-logic" in which the Stranger is the immanent identity of each Human being. The Slave for Wilderson is similarly constitutive of the Human insofar as it gives birth to the World and the Self/Other dynamic. Anthony Paul Smith further echoes this argument by saying that "to be a Stranger to oneself is not to be an Other to oneself, but to be without any stable reference point in the world, to be separated ultimately through one's radical immanence (to oneself) from the world." (Smith 2016, 103) The Stranger-Subject as the Slave is the radical Identity of the Unconscious insofar as it takes the lived experience of history into account. The (Black) non-analyst must be the immanent identity of the philosophical subject that lives in history so as to be constantly working on the latter's desires as transcendental material from the perspective of immanent loss.

I am not here arguing that the (Black) Human *being* and the White Human *being* are identical, even in the last instance. What I am arguing is that the Stranger-Self of the White restrained Unconscious is the (Black) generalized Unconscious. The latter is not the Other of the White restrained Unconscious, but rather the immanent identity of the Unconscious (to) itself when it opens itself up to the desires of (Blackness) by ending the World, since (Blackness), since the Stranger do not exist *in* the World, but rather sees the desires of the World from its perspective.

Laruelle argues that "The closure of the Unconscious by the symptom-form in turn falls into the generalized Unconscious, and this symptom-form (including the other "forms") is no longer merely the object of a displacement and of a restrained analysis, but of an *emplacement* (my italics) by the universal or abstract Unconscious and of a dualysis that transforms it into simple material." (Laruelle 1989, 521) Instead of functioning by displacement or condensation, through the end of the World, there is an *emplacement* from the point of view or according to the (Black) generalized Unconscious. This is not an *emplacing into* as if the White restrained Unconscious were "larger" than the (Black) generalized Unconscious, but rather a postural change of perspective wherein the former is a site or location of analysis for the latter. There is a certain indication of the "placing-in" of foreign desires, desires that are not my own. The desires that come from the perspective of the (Black) non-analyst are far more opaque and expansive. They are not immediately the desires of my Ego, but they are the desires of the Stranger or Slave that is the immanent identity of my transcendental Self and Other, insofar as it takes world-history into account in the last instance. Thus, the desires of the Self and Other, the White restrained Unconscious, are seen as One from the perspective from the (Black) non-analyst. As Laruelle argues in his short essay "Universe Black in Human Foundations of Colour", "The [Black] Universe isn't the object of thought, a greater object than the World; it is thought's *how* or its *according to.*" (Laruelle 1988, 402) The universe is far larger than the World, far more opaque, a superposition of wave and particle. To see *according to* perspective of the (Black) non-analyst is to see from the Vision-in-One. From this perspective the (Black) non-analyst "works" on the metaphysical desires of the White restrained Unconscious, the desires outlined above as "normal desires". In this sense, as Laruelle himself and his commentators have noted, Non-Philosophy, and in this case Non-Analysis is not a *negation* of psychoanalysis but rather its *expansion or dualysis* in the sense that one would use the phrase "Non-Euclidean". Thus, "a generalized analysis necessarily re-introduces into the sphere of analysis everything excluded, therefore psychoanalysis itself and as such with the ensemble of its decisions of the "non-analyzable." (Laruelle 1989, 520) There is therefore an expansion of desires of the White restrained Unconscious from the perspective of the (Black) non-analyst, since the latter expands the analyzable range of the former.

Wilderson argues that the metaphysical position of the "Savage" or indigenous peoples is partially constituted by genocide and sovereignty since the Savage's desires are that of reclaiming a lost sovereignty to the land taken from them. However, it is clear, that from the perspective of the White restrained Unconscious, this desire for a reclaiming of some kind sovereignty other than metaphysical is made but a pathological desire, one that cannot fall within the metaphysical sovereignty of Whiteness. In this sense "the (genocidal immunity) of Whiteness jettisons the White/Red relation from that of a conflict and marks it as an antagonism: it stains it with irreconcilability. Here the Indian comes into being and is positioned by an a priori violence of genocide." (Wilderson 2010, 49) Seeing from the perspective of the (Black) non-analyst as the identity immanent to the generalized Unconscious, it works on the White restrained Unconscious so that the Savage's desire becomes a *semi-metaphysical desire* capable of being desired and realized. This is a desire that cannot appear within the restrained losses of White metaphysical sovereignty. But since seeing from the point of view of the (Black) non-analyst puts them into chaos, new desires from the perspective of the One are introduced. Proceeding from this perspective (Black) non-analyst, there is the possibility of replacing the White restrained Unconscious with a Multi-Racial Unconscious.

(Blackness) insofar as it appears as the (Black) non-analyst immanent to the (Black) generalized Unconscious or the Stranger-Subject already exists outside the World as immanent identity by virtue of its loss, which is why the desire to end the World is the necessary movement that allows the White restrained Unconscious to see from the perspective of the (Black) generalized Unconscious. Insofar as this is true (Blackness) is the minimal perspective for a radical subjectivity, and the minimal perspective for freedom and the articulation of new desires that are seen as One from the point of view of the (Black) non-analyst in the last instance.

Nicholas Eppert, M.A., New York University, Department of Media, Culture and Communication, naeppert[at]gmail.com

References

Barber, Daniel Colucciello. "World-Making and Grammatical Impasse," *Qui Parle* Vol. 25, Nos. 1&2 (Fall/Winter 2016): 179-206.

Fanon, Frantz. *Black Skin, White Masks*. Trans. Philipp Markmann. New York: Grove Press, 2008.

Kolozova, Katherina. "The Inhuman and the Automaton: Exploitation and the Exploited in the Era of Late Capitalism," in *Superpositions: Laruelle and the Humanities*. Ed. Rocco Gangle and Julius Greve. Rowman and Littlefield International Ltd., 2017. 91-102.

Laruelle, Francois. "Universe Black in the Human Foundations of Colour," in McKay, Robin (ed.). *From Decision to Heresy: Experiments in Non-Standard Thought*. Falmouth: Urbanomic, 2012. 402-408.

Laruelle, Francois. "Le concept d'analyse generalisée ou de "non-analyse", *Revue Internationale de Philosophie* Vol. 43, No. 171 (4): 506-524.

Laruelle, Francois. *Theorie des Etrangers: Sciences des Hommes, Democratie, Non-Psychoanalyse*. Paris: Editions Kime, 1995.

Laruelle, Francois. *Dictionary of Non-Philosophy*. Trans. Taylor Adkins. Minneapolis: Univocal Publishing, 2013.

Laruelle, Franois. *Intellectuals and Power*. Trans. Anthony Paul Smith. Polity Press, 2015a.

Laruelle, Francois. *General Theory of Victims*. Trans. Jessie Hock and Alex Dubilet. Polity Press, 2015b.

Marriott, David. *Haunted Life: Visual Culture and Black Modernity*. New Brunswick, New Jersey, and London: Rutgers University Press, 2007.

Sexton, Jared. "The Social Life of Social Death: On Afro-Pessimism and Black Optimism," in *InTensions Journal* Issue 5, (Fall/Winter 2011): 1-47.

Sexton, Jared. "On Black Negativity, or the Affirmation of Nothing," Jared Sexton Interviewed by Daniel Colucciello Barber in *Society+Space*. September 18, 2017. Web. <http://societyandspace.org/2017/09/18/on-black-negativity-or-the-affirmation-of-nothing/>

Smith, Anthony Paul. *Laruelle: A Stranger Thought.* Polity Press, 2016.

Spillers, Hortense J. "'All the Things You Could Be by Now, If Sigmund Freud's Wife Was Your Mother": Psychoanalysis and Race," in Abel, Elizabeth, Barbara Christian, and Helene Moglen (eds.). *Female Subjects in Black and White. Race, Psychoanalysis, Feminism*. Berkeley, Los Anegeles, London: University of California Press, 1997. 135-158.

Warren, Calvin. "Onticide: Afro-pessimism, ~~Gay~~ Nigger #1, and Surplus Violence," in *GLQ: A Journal of Lesbian and Gay Studies* 23:3, (2017): 391-418.

Wilderson. Frank. *Red, White & Black: Cinema and the Structure of U.S. Antagonisms.* Durham & London: Duke University Press, 2010.

Wilderson, Frank. "'We're trying to destroy the world': Anti-Blackness & Police Violence After Ferguson. An Interview with Frank B. Wilderson, III," Interview by Jared Ball, Todd Steven Burroughs and Dr. Hate, *Ill Will Editions* (November 2014): 5-23.

Philosophy, Non-Philosophy, and Performance

LAURA CULL Ó MAOILEARCA (Surrey)

From the Philosophy of Theatre to Performance Philosophy: Laruelle, Badiou and the Equality of Thought

---

Abstract

This article draws from François Laruelle's non-standard philosophy to locate gestures of philosophical "authority" or 'sufficiency" within recent work in the philosophy of theatre – including material from contemporary Anglo-American philosophical aesthetics, and texts by Alain Badiou, such as In Praise of Theatre *(2015). Whilst Badiou initially appears magnanimous in relation to theatre's own thinking – famously describing theatre as "an event of thought" that "directly produces ideas" (Badiou 2005: 72) – I argue that this very benevolence, from a Laruellean perspective, constitutes another form of philosophical authoritarianism. In contrast, I indicate some affinities between Laruelle's non-standard aesthetics and the emerging field of Performance Philosophy – one aim of which, as distinct from the philosophy* of *theatre, would be to allow performance to qualitatively extend our concepts of thinking and/or to be attentive to the ways in which performance has already provided new forms of philosophy.*

Keywords: Laruelle, Badiou, theatre, performance, performance philosophy

---

Introduction:
Laruelle, (non-standard) theatre and performance philosophy

The work of François Laruelle has not yet been extensively taken up by researchers working within the field of Theatre and Performance, at least not in the Anglophone domain. And, perhaps, this will not come as a surprise since, thus far, Laruelle has preferred to use photography, sculpture and music as the material for his non-standard aesthetics, rather than the performing arts. That is, apart from a brief excursus on dance written in 1993 (Laruelle and Edlebi 2013) – which, even then, is concerned with the relation between photography and dance – Laruelle has not explicitly written about theatrical performance in a manner that might attract the field's attention. And yet, an expanded concept of performance – which includes but also extends beyond the performing arts – and the attendant notion of the performative, are clearly core concerns of the Laruellean project, particularly in terms of its emphasis on philosophy itself as an immanent, performative practice that operates "according to" the Real rather than as a transcendent description of it. Indeed, Laruelle characterises thought as "a style, a posture" (Laruelle 2013a, xxi), a bodily "stance" (ibid., 85) or as a matter of "comportment" (ibid., 23), in a manner that suggests a connection to the embodied arts of performance. As philo-fiction, for instance, non-philosophy operates as a non-representational mode of performance – a form of invention that is both immanent and real, rather than a performance or fictionalizing "of" some prior reality. Or, as Laruelle puts it: "To the widespread question: what is it to think?, non-philosophy responds that thinking is not 'thought,' but performing, and that to perform is to clone the world 'in-Real'" (Laruelle 2012a, 233).

At the same time, we might also begin to explore the relationship between Laruelle and theatre by noting his use of a theatrical metaphor to expand upon the core "discovery" and controversial claim of non-philosophy: namely, the universality of what he calls "the Principle of Sufficient Philosophy (PSP)" in his 2011 book, *Anti-Badiou*. Here he argues:

> Philosophy is fundamentally a theatre that denies itself as such, that cannot recognize itself as final duplicity, as a tragedy and a comedy of self repetition. A deus ex machina: the philosopher seems to disappear into philosophy, but in reality projects himself specularly, like a curious god contemplating this game. (Laruelle 2013a, 210)

Moving on to Alain Badiou's philosophy in particular, he then suggests that:

> Materialism begins to simplify the theatre: the philosopher is still necesary – no longer as a god, but in the wings, where he hides himself so as to pull the strings of matter and thought, of Being and consciousness. In materialism, the double or duplicitous philosopher still partitions himself out into two roles; or divides himself.... He is a determinate thought that receives truths without being able to create them, but he is also this meta-ontologue of mathematical Being, this weakened philosopher at the service of mathematical matter, who helps to produce truths. (ibid., 210)

He also aligns non-philosophy with a process of "de-theatricalization", proposing that:

> We must de-theatricalize the scenarios of the imagination. It is not a matter of a foundation of possible scenarios, but of the real scenario fabricated in the undergoing, that real scenario of which all philosophical scenarios are but models. (ibid., 210)

Of course, there is a long history of the use of theatrical metaphor as a means to understand the nature of reality, thought and philosophy – metaphors that obviously vary widely in their implications depending on how "theatre" or theatricality are construed therein. Here, it seems, philosophy is a theatre insofar as it is a "doubling", for Laruelle (Laruelle 2013a, xxvii); what standard philosophy and theatre have in common is the gesture of transcendence and withdrawal that he calls "decision". In this respect, there is the strong impression that the gesture that Laruelle calls "philosophy" – its decisional architecture – has much in common with the position over and above the stage assumed by the figure of the authoritarian, transcendent director. And indeed, as we"ll see in what follows, Badiou's philosophy of theatre – in particular – is a theatrical philosophy in this sense: one that assumes a transcendent position from which to make "a dogmatic unilateral cut between two terms" (Laruelle 2013a, 71) and in so doing reinstates an inequality between philosophical and theatrical knowledges. Despite his apparent descent from the heights of the author-god to the sidelines of the wings, Badiou is like a duplicitous actor, preserving a superior power for philosophy in the very act of seeming to concede it.

But if Laruelle's thought has not yet infiltrated Theatre and Performance, it has already been influential in the emerging field known as "Performance Philosophy": an interdisciplinary field of thought, creative practice and scholarship interrogating the relationship between philosophy and performance broadly construed[1]. Rather than a sub-field of (particularly philosophically-engaged) Theatre and Performance Studies, or a marginal branch of extant Philosophy, Performance Philosophy has sought to cultivate itself as a genuinely independent domain, attempting to foster a community not only of academics but professional practitioners working across a range of contexts including but not limited to institutional ones. As Tony Fisher puts it, "performance philosophy is not just yet *another* philosophy any more than it is just another re-launching of performance theory" (Fisher 2015, 177). Laruelle's work has been attractive to this new field, and indeed has explicitly informed (as well as perhaps behaviourally oriented) aspects of its self-development for a

---

[1] Founded in 2012, Performance Philosophy is also the name of an international research network for the emerging field. The network runs a biennial conference, an open access journal, and a book series (see: http://www.performancephilosophy.org/).

range of reasons – not least insofar as it enacts a welcome deflation of the presumptions of philosophy to theorise the supposedly "non-theoretical art work" (Galloway 2012, 231). The very call for a "performance philosophy" rather than a philosophy *of* performance is – in some respects – a direct response to Laruelle's call for "an art of thought rather than a thought about art", though there are other genealogies too that have led us to this emphasis on thought as real creation (Laruelle 2013b, 5). More expansively, Performance Philosophy benefits from non-philosophy in three key intersecting ways (which, perhaps, are "really" only one): to support i) its critique of "application" – whether in terms of philosophers" circular interpretations of artistic examples or practitioners approaching art-making as an illustrative activity; ii) its consideration of "performance as philosophy" and/or ""the arts" as forms of (non-philosophical) thought"; and iii) its concern with "philosophy as performance" and/or "the arts of philosophy (non-philosophy as performances that *use* philosophy)" (Ó Maoilearca 2015a, 262).

I first came across Laruelle's work through my partner, John Ó Maoilearca, and along with other conveners of the Performance Philosophy research network, like Will Daddario (2015), I have increasingly seen parallels and sympathies between the aims and values of this new field and Laruelle's non-standard philosophy (see Cull 2012, 2014). Correlatively, we might note the engagement with Laruelle by a number of other researchers working in and alongside the performance philosophy context, such as: Tony Fisher (2015, 2017), Tero Nauha (2017a, 2017b), and Hannah Lammin[2]. Nauha, for instance, examines the relationship between non-standard philosophy and performance art practice, developing the concept of what he calls "non-standard artistic research" (Nauha 2017a). For his part, Fisher suggests that my own reading of performance philosophy alongside Laruelle's notion of the "democracy of thought" indicates "the radical ambition of performance philosophy", even though "the scope of that ambition has perhaps not yet been fully assayed, interrogated or understood" (Fisher 2015, 176). Productively though (for our purposes here), Fisher goes on to ask:

> If "non-philosophy" or non-standard philosophy, as Laruelle somtimes calls it, is not itself a philosophy so much as it is the practice of re-orientating philosphy to this

---

[2] Though not yet published, Hannah Lammin has recently completed a PhD entitled, *Staging Community: A Non-Philosophical Presentation of Immanent Social Experience*, which uses Laruelle to re-vision the notion of community in Bataille and Nancy, working towards the articulation of a non-standard model of theatre.

"non-philosophical" margin in a non-appropriative way, then might not performance philosophy be the procedure of introducing democracy into "theories" of performance in order to dissolve their own transcendental status? (Fisher 2015, 181)

However – if readers will forgive the seeming nepotism – John Ó Maoilearca's work (2015a, 2015b) is particularly important here in as much as as it provides the most extensive analysis thus far of the relationship between Laruelle's thought and notions of performance[3]. That is, whilst a great many authors have already noted the important role that notions of performance, embodiment, and the performative, including performative language, play in Laruelle's thought, these themes are given particularly expansive treatment in Ó Maoilearca's *All Thoughts Are Equal*, in which a chapter is devoted to looking at "non-philosophy as a model of performance art" (Ó Maoilearca 2015a, 247), as one performative take – alongside others – on non-philosophy's own performativity. Here performance art – particularly that which works with ordinary actions or quotidian movement as its material (such as the work of American artist, Allan Kaprow) – is presented as one of a set of "real alternatives to standard philosophy" (ibid., 268). Contra the disembodied status assumed by standard philosophy, *All Thoughts Are Equal* seeks to thematize or demonstrate "the postural embodiment of ideas as performance" (ibid., 269). This is significant for Performance Philosophy in many ways, but partly because the field also seeks to provide a place in which to examine not just what philosophers *say*, but what they *do* by saying it (and say by doing it): what philosophical language performs, including in the cases of speech act philosophies themselves which all too often seek to essentialize performativity as activity and action, at the expense of a potentially radical passivity (ibid., 245): "a performed-without-performation" (ibid., 254). Non-philosophy, Ó Maoilearca suggests, calls attention to the "*actual* performance *immanent in this* act of philosophy here and now (doing in saying and saying in doing)" contra philosophical discourses *on* performativity or theatricality which fail to acknowledge themselves as performance, as a form of art rather than authoritative description (ibid., 260).

In this context, my own contribution here uses a selection of recent work from the philosophy of theatre – both "analytic" and "Continental" (in the case of Alain Badiou) – as the material for a Laruellean analysis, exposing and challenging the performative subordination of theatre to philosophy enacted by the texts. In this respect, this article is only a first instantiation of my own wider project, informed by Laruelle's work, seeking to articulate a

---

[3] John Ó Maoilearca is also a founding core convener of the Performance Philosophy network.

potential role for Performance Philosophy in contributing to the "extraordinary flattening" of thinking practices understood as *equally* determined by the Real (Laruelle & Edlebi 2013, 151). This forms part of a collaborative effort to understand Performance Philosophy as a thinking practice aiming to operate not as one more hierarchical order, but to offer "an equality – which owes nothing to the leveling of a prior hierarchy – to the qualitative inequality that makes up the ground of the real" (ibid., 155). It looks towards Performance Philosophy as a potential site in which the qualitative heterogeneity of thought might be "*felt* differently" (ibid., 154). Here, Laruelle figures as a resource through which Performance Philosophy might understand itself: as a place in which to pursue "the utopian hope for a (non-)philosophy that is regarded as an equal to art (qua thought)" (Ó Maoilearca 2015a, 249).

In this way, no doubt, this article will prove unsatisfying in terms of articulating non-standard theatre: what it might mean, in practice, to subject theatre (including the philosophy of theatre, theatre and performance studies, and theatre and performance practice) to a non-standard method. Of course, we know already that it does not mean the *negation* or "mere extension" of theatre (Ó Maoilearca 2015a, 251), but its qualitative mutation and widening according to a material practice that "opens it up to the Real rather than relativizing it into nothing" (ibid., 244).

Likewise, we are yet to really think through what non-philosophy means for how fields like theatre and performance engage with philosophy and "theory". In the first instance though, perhaps, it means a commitment to the ongoing work required to equalize, level or flatten out the persistent hierarchies of relation that serve to structure encounters between the objects, practices and practitioners of theatre and philosophy respectively – overriding, for instance, the false distinction of "theory" and "practice". Like many other arts and humanities disciplines, at least in the UK context, theatre and performance has been through a series of theoretical phases or "trends" wherein particular branches of Continental European philosophy (and it is almost always "Continental" rather than Anglo-American) are enthusiastically taken up as the next new framework through which the "object" of performance might be understood, the next new method which might be adapted and adopted either by practitioners as the lens through which to view their own practice or by those scholars seeking to bring fresh eyes to the act of performance analysis. If there have been periods where a broadly Derridean outlook was *de rigueur*, followed by – in some areas – a prevalence of the Deleuzian model, recent years have seen a growing engagement with so-called "new materialism", amongst other currently fashionable paradigms. In contrast, commentators have been at pains to emphasis that Laruelle is not "the next big thing" (Mullarkey and Smith 2012, 1) in Continental philosophy, such that those in theatre and performance research who consider themselves "in the know", theoretically, must feel obliged to show an interest in and familiarity with his ideas. There would be a deep irony if the effect of this kind of article was to suggest to theatre makers that they need to read Laruelle in order to better understand their art. On the contrary, to arts practitioners, Laruelle's project seems to signal a welcome modesty insofar as it insists that: "Non-philosophy is not 'the highest' exercise of thought; this no longer means anything for a non-philosophy which does not know the 'superior form" of thought." (Laruelle 2013c, 197) Rather, the productive indefinition or underdetermination of philosophy by non-philosophy (Ó Maoilearca 2015a, 244) seems to open the way for renewed attempts to consider "theatre *as* philosophy", "dance *as* philosophy", "music *as* philosophy" but not according to some identification (or motivated by any sense of a need for any vicarious intellectual justification), so much as with a view to the invention of new forms of philosophy (which would also be the discovery of forms of philosophy in performance *that were already there*).

1. The philosophy of theatre

The last 20 years have seen a growth of literature in both the analytic and Continental philosophy of theatre. In terms of the former, Paul Thom's 1993 book *For An Audience* used to be the only monograph specifically looking at theatre from an analytic perspective. But in recent years we have seen a host of new texts appear such that in 2009, Nöel Carroll felt justified to pronounce: "After decades of neglect… the philosophy of theater is back in business" (Carroll 2009, 441). Whilst Carroll was thinking specifically of the neglect of theatre by Anglo-American philosophy, it is independently true that theatre has been sidelined by Continental European philosophy as well – with Badiou, for instance, describing it as "the ugly duckling" among the arts (Badiou 2013, 207)[4]. Here too though there appears to have been a shift:

---

[4] However, Timothy Murray's important edited collection *Mimesis, Masochism & Mime* (1997) was the first to register an emerging discourse around "the role of theatricality in critical thought" in French philosophy since the 1970s – drawing together key essays by Cixous, Deleuze, Derrida, Foucault, Irigaray amongst others. At that time though, as Murray notes, the focus on theatricality was

with contemporary philosophers from Rancière, Cixous and Žižek as well as Badiou all devoting significant attention to theatre.

However, whilst such philosophical attention is welcome in some respects, it seems fair to say that much of this new philosophy of theatre is marked by some fairly conservative tendencies in terms of its representation and understanding of theatre. Let me note three of these to begin with. Firstly, this philosophy of theatre is focussed almost exclusively on the work of individual white, male, European playwrights[5]. Secondly, the theatre "proper" – the norm or centre in relation to which all other practices are measured – is predominantly identified with drama or the staging of plays and, for the most part, theatre is defined as clearly distinct from dance, cinema and indeed theatrical events in everyday life (with the exception of Paul Woodruff) – in a manner that stands in stark contrast to the interdisciplinary nature of contemporary practices. And thirdly, in this work, philosophy tends to set itself up as being in a position of power and authority in relation to theatre – for instance, as uniquely positioned to produce an authoritative knowledge of theatre's ontology. This latter issue is at the heart of this article and one that I seek to address through an engagement with Laruelle.

My own current project – very much a "work in progress" – attempts to draw from Laruelle's non-philosophy and particularly his notion of non-standard aesthetics, firstly to critique the operation of philosophical authority within these contemporary philosophies of theatre, but then also to develop an alternative paradigm: a "performance philosophy" rather than a philosophy of performance; a style of thought that is in a continuous process of rethink-

---

less an indication of philosophical concern with "avant-garde developments" on the stage, and more with theatricality as a route into the discussion of "broader issues of representation". That is, whilst some of these philosophers did engage with contemporary theatre practices (if we think of Deleuze with Carmelo Bene, for instance; and more significantly Cixous' ongoing collaborations with Ariane Mnouchkine), Murray's sense is that the primary concern of this work was really with "the structural and epistemological status of mimesis (imitation)" (Murray 1997: 1).

[5] For instance, one might observe that in Tom Stern's recent book (2014), *Philosophy and theatre: an introduction*, the philosophy of theatre is predominantly limited to the discussion of canonical Western, white, male playwrights: Shakespeare, Chekhov, and Brecht (with Caryl Churchill as the only contemporary and female artist referenced). Likewise, Badiou's own theatrical pantheon is made up almost exclusively of individual (white, male, European) playwrights. His latest text on theatre, *In Praise of Theatre* sees the philosopher sticking fairly closely to his usual list of 'great dramatists': Chekhov, Ibsen, O'Neill, the symbolist theatre of Claudel, Brecht, Pirandello. The contemporary director and co-founder of the Pandora Company, Brigitte Jaques is mentioned once in passing (Badiou and Truong 2015, 4). Likewise, the preceding volume, *Rhapsody for the Theatre* the key exalted references are as above, along with Mallarmé, Vitez, Racine, Beckett, Genet, and Sean O'Casey.

ing itself and of expanding its own definition, insofar as it thinks *alongside* rather than about performance's thinking, which is itself an equal part of the Real.

ll too often, I suggest, the philosophy of theatre seems to embark on its encounter with the field of theatre and performance sure in its knowledge of what it means to think – philosophically, theatrically, fundamentally – and authorizing its own privileged capacity to represent the nature of thought. Inspired but by no means authorized by Laruelle, an alternative, immanentist and pluralist approach might begin from the hypothetical stance: "if performance is thinking, then what does that do to my understanding of thought?" To clarify: to say that performance is its "own" kind of thinking here, is not to posit some fundamental distinction between this thought and philosophy's – an identification that could only be made by presuming to know what makes philosophy what it is. Speaking in terms of performance's own thought, is rather an attempt to clarify that this is not a call for performance to be included in any dominant definition of thought, to be recognized as measuring up to whatever counts as thought in a given situation, so much as a call for a genuine democratization of the category of thought itself, for performance to be treated as an equal participant in an ongoing mutation and multiplication of thought's possibilities.

2. Laruelle & non-standard aesthetics

As we know, Laruelle's work aims to democratize or equalize the relationship that philosophy has to other forms of thought, including the arts. His non-philosophical project is an attempt to perform a qualitative extension of the category of thought without any one kind of thinking positioning itself as its exemplary form that, therefore, is in a position to police the inclusion and exclusion or relative status of other thoughts within the category. The discipline of Philosophy has often sought to play this authoritarian role, Laruelle claims. For Laruelle, standard philosophy involves the gesture wherein thought withdraws from the world in order to occupy a position of authority or power in relation to it. Or as he puts it: "To philosophise on X is to withdraw from X; to take an essential distance from the term for which we will posit other terms" (Laruelle 2012b, 229). In contrast, in *Principles of Non-Philosophy*, for instance, Laruelle asks us to consider how we might equalize philosophy and art, "outside of every hierarchy" (Laruelle 2013a, 289). Laruelle argues that "we must first change the very concept of thought, in its relations to philosophy and to other forms of knowledge" (Laruelle 2012b, 232). According to this democracy of thinking, the call is not "to think without philosophy but to think without the authority of philosophy"

(Laruelle 2006, np). Through a non-philosophical procedure, philosophy and theatre would be realigned as equal yet different forms of thought – embedded in the whole of the Real, with neither being granted any special powers to exhaust the nature of the other, nor indeed the nature of the whole in which they take part.

For some, philosophy's sense of its own universal applicability is both a source of pride and indicative of its disciplinary exceptionalism. However, in Laruelle's non-philosophy, this same characteristic is the source of critique. As Ó Maoilearca suggests in *All Thoughts are Equal*, "Whereas standard philosophical approaches take their conception of what proper philosophy is and then apply it to all and sundry objects—which Laruelle calls the "Principle of Sufficient Philosophy"– non-philosophy is a 'style of thought" that mutates with its object" (Ó Maoilearca 2015a, 13). However, it seems important to emphasise that what Laruelle calls "philosophy" is a tendency that – although it has often been performed (differently) by the discipline of Philosophy – can also be found in other disciplinary fields, like Theatre and Performance. In this sense, when Laruelle critiques "philosophy" he is not exclusively criticizing the discipline of Philosophy in its various historical and institutional formations – albeit that non-philosophy has particularly focused its experiments on materials associated with European traditions within Philosophy. Rather, what Laruelle calls "philosophy" is a transcendental gesture within thought in which it assumes its "primacy… over all knowledge" (Laruelle 2013b, 37).

And just as Laruelle's non-philosophy more broadly aims to deprive philosophy of its sufficiency and authority regarding the "democracy of thought" that, for him, constitutes the indeterminable and inexplicable nature of the real, he specifically seeks to deprive aesthetics of "its sufficiency vis-à-vis art" (Laruelle 2013b, 2). "There is a Principle of Sufficient Aesthetics derived from the Principle of Sufficient Philosophy" (ibid., 3) – for instance when aesthetics assumes a transcendent position from which to determine the necessary and sufficient conditions for art. In contrast, Laruelle describes his own "non-aesthetics" or "non-standard aesthetics" as "another solution that, without excluding aesthetics, no longer grants it this domination of philosophical categories over works of art, but limits it in order to focus on its transformation", aiming toward "the reciprocal determination of art and philosophy" (ibid., 1).

Based on this preliminary introduction, Laruelle's concept of a non-standard aesthetics might not sound substantially different from the kinds of appeals to the autonomy of art from philosophy and the critique of the logic of recognition that we find in thinkers like

Deleuze and Badiou. Laruelle is, of course, by no means the first to call for something like a philosophy *from* art rather than a philosophy *of* art. Indeed, Laruelle himself refers to Deleuze's Spinozist call to "create concepts parallel to artistic works" as a "giant step toward a non-standard aesthetics" (Laruelle 2013b, 6). And yet, there are some subtle differences between these enterprises. For instance, Laruelle suggests that both Deleuze and Badiou ultimately end up over-determining the nature of art's thought from the point of view of their own philosophy, even whilst they characterise it as external to it. That is, insofar as Deleuze is willing to define the force of art in terms of *affect* (relative to philosophy's concepts and science's functions), he still performatively claims a privileged epistemological status for (his own) philosophy. Art cannot produce "encounters" – cannot transform Deleuze's thought – to the extent that it is over-determined as encounter qua the forcing of thought by difference. Likewise, as we"ll see later on this article, Badiou's characterization of theatre as a "generic truth procedure" (that conditions philosophy rather than functioning as its object) ostensibly removes philosophy's ontological function (which Badiou assigns to set theory as a privileged ontology of the pure multiple), but covertly conserves its authority through this very meta-ontological gesture. So, in this sense, whilst it may be increasingly commonplace to *say* that what we want is something like a "performance philosophy" rather than a "philosophy *of* performance", it is often harder to put such an equality of thought into practice.

3. The analytic philosophy of theatre

Starting with the analytic or Anglo-American philosophy of theatre, one example of how philosophical "authority" or 'sufficiency" manifests itself is in the often rigid and unilateral approach to the definition of theatre. This is superficially evident in the titles given to chapters in some of these books, which are called things like: "What Theater Is" (Woodruff 2008), "What Actors Do" (Zamir 2014) or "What performers do and what audiences can know" (Hamilton 2007). But more substantially, we might suggest that philosophy assumes a position of transcendent authority in relation to theatre when it assigns itself an exceptional, ontological capacity to clarify what kind of "thing" theatre is, what type of thing a play is, what makes *Hamlet Hamlet* and so on. One particular strand of this is the "obsession" with what counts as "the work of art" in the context of theatre and performance and/or addressing the identity of theatre in terms of the text/performance relationship. Very much in line with analytic philosophies of music and dance, discussion of theatre in analytic aesthetics often takes the form of attempts to determine what constitutes a theatrical "work": is it the dramatic text, all performances which are "faithful" to the text, any performance that gets near to fidelity or authenticity, or can there be performances without texts? Questions of theatre ontology, play identity and authentic performance lead to debates as to the conditions that must be satisfied in order for two difference performances to count as instances of the 'same" work. Of course, analytic philosophers of theatre hold a range of views on this point – from those, like Paul Woodruff, who argue that there is some "thing" – the performable work – which is repeated by but irreducible to its productions and performances of those productions (Woodruff 2008, 57), to those like James R. Hamilton (2007) who reject the very idea that performances are "of" anything extraneous to them. But what does not vary, arguably, is the assumed capacity of philosophy to define theatre, and yet not be defined by it reciprocally.

Here analytic philosophers have applied the well-worn ontological distinction between general "types" and their concrete "tokens" to the relationship between dramatic text and theatrical performance – oftentimes assuming for their own thought the role of gatekeeper with respect to the criteria (or "fidelity standards") for a true performance of X; philosophy nominates itself as in a position to determine what allows a given performance to be a "correct", "authentic" or otherwise "properly formed token" of a given work; what makes one interpretation more truthful to the work than another. Gatekeepers against relativism: "We must not let just anything be called *Hamlet*" (Woodruff 2008, 52) – Woodruff warns.

But whether or not they think this relationship in Platonic terms – of philosophy as capable of seeing beyond the material appearance of tokens (performances) to the ideal types (works) they instantiate – what remains unchanged, from a Laruellean perspective, is the auto-positioning of the philosopher as transcendent authority. In this respect, I am less concerned about the hierarchy between *text and performance* which the analytic philosophy of theatre has relentlessly sought to address, and more concerned with the hierarchy between *philosophy and theatre*: between the mode of thought and knowledge that the philosophy of theatre assumes for itself and that which it assigns to theatre (with *the very act of assignation* being a moot point). That is, whilst the analytic philosophy of theatre has developed its own extensive critique of the idea that a performance is necessarily a "performance of X" (*of* an independent work, such as a play-text, and all the issues of hierarchy and determination that such a model has tended to imply in terms of the relationship between text and performance)[6], there arguably remains limited attention to the forms of power and evaluation involved in the philosophical definition of the identity of theatre itself.

4. Badiou's philosophy of theatre

Now, these issues are not exclusive to the analytic philosophy of theatre. In comparison to the material introduced above, we might be initially hopeful that Badiou's engagement with the theatrical field might avoid philosophical authoritarianism. It is he, after all, who lays out as first principle in his "Theses on Theater" the need to establish "that theater thinks" (Badiou 2005, 72). Here, he famously describes theatre as "an event of thought" and as an event that "directly produces ideas" (ibid.). Likewise, in *Rhapsody for the Theatre*, he states: "I am convinced that theatre in and of itself, through its own resources, constitutes a particularly active form of thought, an act of thought. It is, as Mallarmé used to say, a 'superior" art" (Badiou 2013, 290). And yet, as we"ll see, Badiou ultimately positions himself as the authority on the kind of thought that theatre is (as truth-procedure for instance), the nature of the relationship between that thought and philosophy, and as the one who can bestow upon mathematics the honour of exemplifying thought in its highest form.

As is well known, Badiou describes philosophy as conditioned by four, non-philosophical forms of thought or "generic truth-procedures": art, politics, science and love. In their true or proper forms – which are inevitably rare, for Badiou – each of these procedures involves the production of truths, and the co-engendering of "events" and 'subjects". According to Badiou, philosophy itself does not produce truth; this is solely the remit of the four procedures. In contrast, it is the exclusive function of philosophy to 'subtract" or 'seize" the truths generated by the fields that condition it, such as theatre.

In this context, Badiou argues that theatre in its true form, is a theatre of Ideas but one that is "irreducible to philosophy" (Badiou 2005, 9). So theatre thinks, for Badiou; but it does not think *philosophically*. Rather, he is insistent that what theatre produces are resolutely "*theater-ideas*": thoughts that "cannot be produced in any other place or by any other means",

---

[6] For example, both David Saltz and James Hamilton are not only critical of textual priority in the literary model, but also in the subsequent 'the two-text model' – as employed in much semiotic theory wherein the performance itself is conceived as a 'text' that transforms, translates or 'transcodes' a written text – for failing to escape fidelity standards and maintaining a Platonic hierarchy of text as original type and performance as poor copy (Saltz 1995: 266; Hamilton 2007: 27).

including by philosophy, and thoughts that do not pre-exist their staging as theatrical event (Badiou 2005, 72). For Badiou, Kenneth Reinhard suggests, theatre "is the condition of possibility for a kind of truth to which we would otherwise have no access" (Reinhard 2013, xxv). This separation is a necessary consequence of Badiou's definition of philosophy as conditioned insofar as the capacity of the four truth procedures to produce the radical rupture with existing knowledge can only occur, for him, to the extent that they are understood as heterogeneous and external to philosophy. Recalling Deleuze's notion of encounter, theatre can only make philosophy think if its own thinking is that which philosophy cannot recognize according to its existing schemas. And in turn, to reassert the specifically Badiouian dimension of this proposition: when theatre thinks, what it produces (albeit often unwittingly according to Badiou) are events of truth that depend upon the philosopher to seize and be seized by them, as well as upon other subjects (audiences, other theatre-makers) who are produced as such to the extent that they faithfully pursue the implications of the events they have witnessed.

So theatre thinks but is not philosophy, for Badiou. In this respect, Badiou presents himself as denouncing any illustrative function for the theatre and, correlatively, any parasitic invasion of theatre by philosophy. In turn, he advocates for what he calls "inaesthetics" – as distinct from conventional philosophical aesthetics – as a mode of relation between art and philosophy wherein the latter does not claim to think for art, recognizes that "art is itself a producer of truths", and "makes no claim to turn it into an object for philosophy" (Badiou 2005, xxvii).

But is there a gap between what Badiou says and does here, with respect to addressing the inequalities of conventional approaches to aesthetics? Laruelle's *Anti-Badiou* (2013) suggests as much, identifying a fundamental paradox at the heart of Badiou's work. In his famous formulation, mathematics = ontology, Badiou ostensibly intends to reveal that the pure multiple (as construed in set theory) "can and must be the condition, rather than the object, of "Philosophy""(Laruelle 2013a, xxi). If ontology concerns multiplicity as the nature of being or existence beyond the particularity of how different beings exist, then for Badiou, ontology is best conducted in the form of mathematics as the science of quantities rather than qualities. For Badiou, set theory especially, is also the purest means to think multiplicity or the condition of belonging to a set as what all beings have in common. It presents the universal nature of being (as multiple) because it deals exclusively with quantities or sets of things, rather than with the qualities of the things counted.

In this way, Laruelle suggests, Badiou *appears* to "reduce" philosophy "in its relation to the four "truth procedures," to a simple "inventory" function—that is, to the function of a widened synthesis or weakened (weakly encyclopedic) system" rather than as a source of truth in itself. In ceding to mathematics philosophy's historical self-nomination as the privileged site of ontological knowledge – "the most essential of all knowledges, that of being itself qua being" (Laruelle 2013a, 162) – Badiou *seems* to be performing the sort of flattening gesture of which Laruelle ought to approve. However, Laruelle accuses Badiou of failing to really cede the place of philosophy to mathematics insofar as he assumes for himself a meta-ontological role. The very act of assuming to relieve philosophy of ontology exacts a meta-ontological authority and mastery (ibid., 14), which retains "the primacy of philosophy over all knowledge" (ibid., 37). In the end, Laruelle suggests Badiou responds to the problem of how to conserve philosophy "by amputating its sickly member (the philosophical ontology of "presence") and issuing it with a mathematical prosthesis" (ibid., 17). Equated with set theory, ontology then becomes a special form of "non-philosophy" in the very interior of philosophy" (ibid., 15).

In the same way, we might suggest that whilst in works such as *In Praise of Theatre* (2015), Badiou initially appears magnanimous in relation to theatre's own thinking, and indeed to demote the function of philosophy in relation to an ontological privilege now accorded (*by him*) to set theory, this very benevolence, from a Laruellean perspective, constitutes another form of *philosophical* authoritarianism. That is, whilst Badiou describes theatre as "an event of thought" that "directly produces ideas" (Badiou 2005, 72), he ultimately positions himself as the authority on what "counts as theatre properly speaking" (Badiou 2013, 109); he performatively positions his own thought as normative exception and as the gatekeeper to that exception.

For instance, both in *Rhapsody* and *In Praise of Theatre*, Badiou develops a distinction, between what he calls true Theatre – or Theatre with a capital T – and "theatre". The latter is broadly equated with entertainment and with the reinforcement of conventional opinion. As Badiou puts it, "bad theatre is a collection of established identities, which it works to reproduce with conventional ideas and the corresponding decent opinions which come along with them" (Badiou with Truong 2015, 84). As a consequence, this false theatre fails to make any particular demands of or to change its audience, who Badiou characterizes as homogeneous and yet particular insofar as they share the same limited class or set of opinions, in contrast to the universal audience produced by Theatre (Badiou 2013, 62). In "theatre", Badiou suggests, "nothing has happened to anyone, except sinking into the basest of opinions" (Badiou 2013, 221); rather, small "t" theatre "induces a convivial satisfaction in those who hate truth" (ibid., 62). In contrast, in true Theatre, "we come upon the process of a truth, of an elucidation whose spectacle would be the event" (ibid., 66). True Theatre is never "a phenomenon of opinion": "To the truths, and not to the opinions. Therein lies the force of all genuine theatre. The false theatre, which I call "theatre", by no means represents an encounter with eternity, since it calls upon vulgar opinions; it has no universality, since it is aimed at an audience that is pre-formed by its opinions, most often of a repulsively reactionary nature" (ibid., 220). This distinction also allows Badiou to emphasise the rarity of true Theatre: "there is little, very little Theatre, because "theatre" most often protects us from it." (ibid., 64) False "theatre" can take many forms for Badiou – such as an instance of a mere execution of an existing text with no creative merit, in theatres that involve "copying a dead tradition, of a run-of-the-mill classic" (ibid., 79). But it might also be what Badiou describes as "boulevard theatre" – from "Jean de Létraz to Harold Pinter". This is theatre that is commercially successful and finances itself without state support; highly conventional albeit better packaged than much theatre on the "cultural circuit" (ibid., 58-59), but it is clear that such theatre has no philosophical or political consequences for Badiou.

Subsequently, in *In Praise of Theatre*, Badiou specifically characterises theatre proper as something of an endangered art in our current context: as under threat both from what he describes as both its "right" and "left". Ironically, that is, Badiou suggests that true Theatre is at risk from the exclusive or monopolizing tendencies of the clichéd entertainment of "musical comedies based on the American model" on the one hand (Badiou with Truong 2015, 9-10) and from the anti-representationalist "theatre without theatre" exemplified by Fabre and Castellucci on the other (ibid., 18). That is, he is himself seeking to monopolize theatre when he argues that *what he defines as* "entertainment" complicit with the status quo, and "theatre without theatre" "cannot and must not constitute the whole of the theatre" (ibid., 19). Badiou claims that "All theatre is a theatre of Ideas", but only specifically if we understand "the Idea (in Plato's sense)" (Badiou 2013, 93). As such, this is not to say that all theatre thinks, but rather that, for Badiou, any so-called "theatre" that fails to think according to his model of thought is one that is unworthy of the name.

5. Performance philosophy

To conclude, I want to suggest that the emerging field of Performance Philosophy might be understood as an alternative paradigm to such authoritarian gestures: as an ethico-political project in pursuit of a democracy of thought, including equalizing the performance-philosophy relationship (though crucially not according to some "illustration" of Laruelle). Here, I suggest that the aim of a performance philosophy – as distinct from a philosophy *of* theatre – would be to allow performance to qualitatively extend our concepts of thinking and/or to be attentive to the ways in which performance *has already provided* new forms of philosophy.

From a Laruellean perspective, theatre and philosophy as forms of thought, as well as thought in general, are "perpetually indefinite" in a manner that resists any essentialising definition (Mullarkey 2009, 208, 210). This is not inconsistent or paradoxical, in that to call theatre a perpetually indefinite process is not to provide a definition of it. Nor is it a rejection of the production of definitions of theatre, so much as a call to open the 'stance" we occupy in relation to the multiplicity of definitions produced by the philosophy of theatre, theatre studies and by theatre practice itself. Such a stance does not deny the concrete specificity of different forms of thought; nor does this alternative paradigm involve renouncing the "techniques" belonging to specific practices of philosophy and theatre, in favour of a kind of post-disciplinary or post-professional dilettantism. Indeed, elsewhere, Laruelle suggests that "it is necessary to know what is philosophy and what is science" for instance – but this is necessarily and perpetually a provisional knowledge in a given context (Laruelle 2013a, 71). It is not a knowledge arrived at in advance via a "dogmatic *unilateral cut* between two terms", but one that performs an "ambiguity of relations" (ibid.).

What does this mean for the philosophical project of definition? At times, it does seem as though Laruelle refuses definition outright insofar as he construes definitions as imposing unnecessary limits on the inclusive expansion of both philosophy and thought: "as soon as I give a definition it is a failure. We have to refuse the temptation or appearance of definition" (Laruelle in Ó Maoilearca 2015, 7). And yet, we might suggest that this is specifically a critique of a certain kind of rigid and unilateral definition, rather than the notion of a definitional project *per se*. What matters, as Andrew Bowie (2007) has discussed with respect to music and philosophy, is that we think in terms of a "complex two-way relationship" rather than in terms of a unilateral one in which it is philosophy's role to determine and define (whether masked as "description" or privileged ontological "insight") the nature of theatre practice with no such determination operating in the other direction: *of* philosophy *by* theatre. Or again, what matters is that every definition is provisional and must remain provisional: as a sort of fiction – but by no means "unreal" as such. Definition *is* theatre, then, understood in an expanded and expanding fashion, understood indefinitely, by or through the very performance of thinking it as an equal to philosophy and other forms of thought.

Dr. Laura Cull Ó Maoilearca, Centre for Performance Philosophy,
University of Surrey, UK, l.cull[at]gsa.surrey.ac.uk

References

Badiou, Alain. *Handbook of Inaesthetics*. Translated by Alberto Toscano. Stanford: Stanford University Press, 2005.

Badiou, Alain. *Rhapsody for the Theatre*. Translated by Bruno Bosteels. London/NY: Verso, 2013.

Badiou, Alain with Truong, Nicolas. *In Praise of Theatre*. Translated, with an introduction and notes by Andrew Bielski. Cambridge, UK/Malden, USA: Polity Press, 2015.

Bowie, Andrew. *Music, Philosophy, and Modernity*. Cambridge: Cambridge University Press, 2007.

Carroll, Noël. "On the Necessity of Theater (review)." *Philosophy and Literature* Vol. 33, Nr. 2 (2009): 435-441.

Cull, Laura. "Performance as Philosophy: Responding to the Problem of "Application"." *Theatre Research International* Vol. 37, Nr. 1 (2012): 20-27.

Cull, Laura. "Performance Philosophy – Staging a New Field." in Laura Cull and Alice Lagaay (eds.). *Encounters in Performance Philosophy*. Basingtoke: Palgrave Macmillan, 2014. 15-38.

Daddario, Will. "Doing Life Is That Which We Must Think." in Laura Cull Ó Maoilearca (ed.). *Performance Philosophy* Vol. 1 (2015): 168-174.

Fisher, Tony. "Thinking without Authority: performance philosophy as the democracy of thought," in Laura Cull Ó Maoilearca (ed.). *Performance Philosophy* Vol. 1 (2015): 175-184.

Fisher Tony. "Introduction: Performance and the Tragic Politics of the *Agōn*". in Tony Fisher and Eve Katsouraki (eds.). *Performing Antagonism*. London: Palgrave Macmillan, 2017.

Galloway, Alexander R. "Laruelle and Art". *Continent* Vol. 2, Nr. 4 (2012): 230-236

Hailton, James R. *The Art of Theater*. Oxford: Wiley-Blackwell, 2007.

Laruelle, François, and Alyosha Edlebi. "First Choreography: Or the Essence-of-Dance". *Qui Parle: Critical Humanities and Social Sciences* Vol. 21, Nr. 2 (2013): 143-155.

Laruelle, François. *Anti-Badiou: The Introduction of Maoism into Philosophy*. Translated by Robin Mackay. London and New York: Bloomsbury, 2013a.

Laruelle, François. *Photo-Fiction, a Non-Standard Aesthetics*. Translated by Drew S. Burk. Minneapolis, MN: Univocal, 2013b.

Laruelle, François. Principles of Non-Philosophy, translated by Nicola Rubczak and Anthony Paul Smith. London/New York: Bloomsbury, 2013c.

Laruelle, François. *From Decision to Heresy: Experiments in Non-Standard Thought*. Edited by Robin Mackay. Falmouth, U.K.: Urbanomic/Sequence Press, 2012a.

Laruelle, François. "Is Thinking Democratic?" In John Mullarkey and Anthony Paul Smith (ed.) *Laruelle and Non-Philosophy*, Edinburgh: Edinburgh University Press, 2012b. 227–237.

Laruelle, François. "La lettre de François Laruelle du 30 Mai 2006, "Les effets-Levinas"." Organisation Non-Philosophique Internationale, 2006. Web. 28 April 2017. <http://www.onphi.org/lettre-laruelle----effets-levinas-12.html>

Mullarkey, John. *Refractions of Reality: Philosophy and the Moving Image*. Basingstoke: Palgrave Macmillan, 2009.

Mullarkey, John and Smith, Anthony Paul. *Laruelle and Non-Philosophy*. Edinburgh: Edinburgh University Press, 2012.

Ó Maoilearca, John. *All Thoughts are Equal: Laruelle and Nonhuman Philosophy*. Minneapolis: University of Minnesota Press, 2015a.

Ó Maoilearca, John. "Laruelle's "Criminally Performative" Thought: On Doing and Saying in Non-Philosophy". in Laura Cull Ó Maoilearca (ed.). *Performance Philosophy* Vol. 1 (2015b): 161-167.

Reinhard, Kenneth. "Introduction: Badiou's Theater: A Laboratory for Thinking." in Alain Badiou. *The incident at Antioch: a tragedy in three acts*. Translated by Susan Spitzer. New York: Columbia University Press, 2013. xxi-li.

Stern, Tom. *Philosophy and theatre: an introduction*. Abingdon, Oxon/New York: Routledge, 2014.

Nauha, Tero. "From Schizoproduction to Non-Standard Artistic Research." in Paulo de Assis and Paolo Giudici (eds.). *The Dark Precursor: Deleuze and Artistic Research*. Leuven: Leuven University Press, 2017a. 252-260

Nauha, Tero. "A thought of performance." *Performance Philosophy* Vol. 2, Nr. 2 (2017b): 272-285.

Woodruff, Paul. *The Necessity of Theater: The Art of Watching and Being Watched*. Oxford: Oxford University Press, 2008.

Zamir, Tzachi. *Acts: Theater, Philosophy and the Performing Self*. Ann Arbor: University of Michigan Press, 2014.

GILBERT KIEFFER (Santo Domingo/Kolsko)

La voix du philosophe Laruelle

The Voice of Laruelle, the philosopher
(Abstract)

What is a voice in the context of the arts and philosophy? In the space of the philosopher's voice, in the complex grammar of his language is played his philosophical timbre, his own space, his particular voice, composed of concepts, articulated by the laws of coherence of the common philosophical language, with hypnotic specificities. These specificities are precisely the fruit of processes formerly called rhetoric, which I call non-hypnotics (of generalized hypnotic space), one of whose functions is just to speak in a double space: the common reference space of the reader or listener, and the conceptual virtual space peculiar to the philosopher. To the extent that the reader must pay increased and permanent attention to this double space, the philosophical trance effect, equivalent to the Ericksonian hypnotic trance, is facilitated. The difficulty of this double reading is the incessant passage from one code to another, which is also a hypnotic fascination. Heidegger prolongs and renews its structures and draws some effects from them, which provoke in the mind of the reader as an overflow, a saturation effect, which itself favors the philosophical trance. Thus, each voice seeks to captivate the mind by confusing it with concepts, which seem at first sight familiar, but which reveal themselves with the use which is made, like formidable concepts to the power of unaccustomed fascination. One of the pleasures of reading Lareuelle's philosophy is due to this type of fascination with the philosophical voice and its language.

Keywords: François Laruelle, voice, art, philo-fiction, philosophical opera

---

Qu'est-ce qu'une voix dans le domaine de l'art et de la philosophie ?

Je le dirai de manière proustienne, en ajoutant la réminiscence au déroulement de ma parole. Je le dirai aussi de manière heideggerienne, quelquefois directement en allemand. Je suivrai toujours cette quête de la voix, qui nous parle par l'intermédiaire du livre, à travers les concepts et les mots d'approche, et qui est si difficile à déterminer dans son essence propre.

L'événement qui me motive spécialement est que nous venons d'accueillir, Anetka et moi-même, François Laruelle et Anne-Françoise Schmid en Pologne, pour l'inauguration du

Centre de Kolsko, centre de rencontres et de partages créatifs dans le domaine de la science, de la philosophie et des arts. Nos différentes conversations ont pu aboutir à un thème qui intéressait spontanément, à la fois François Laruelle, et Anne-Françoise Schmid. Il s'agissait de l'idée de "voix", idée peut-être conceptuellement mal exprimée encore, puisqu'elle utilise toujours un mot ancien, auquel elle impose de curieuses torsions. Moi, à ce moment-là j'étais en train d'écrire une paraphrase sur Heidegger dans le style proustien. François Laruelle cherchait à organiser ses 4 livres en un opéra philosophique, sans abandonner l'idée d'une lecture auto-biographique conceptuelle de la vie, de sa vie. Anne-Françoise Schmid développait les *Scripts philosophiques*. Nous avions abordé l'idée que, d'un penseur, d'un écrivain, il devait rester en réalité plus qu'un simple texte, et que ce qu'on ressentait comme "sa voix" était autre chose que le timbre de sa voix réelle, tel qu'elle pouvait subsister dans des enregistrements.

On se demandait alors, par quoi caractériser "une voix" qui nous parle dans ce qu'on lit d'elle ? Comment définir la voix de François Laruelle, par exemple? Si telle voix devait exister, elle ne pourrait pas être "une", commune à toutes nos lectures. Elle devait porter aussi l'inflexion de celui qui la reçoit et la lit, un peu plus loin que le texte qui la porte. J'avais commencé par en définir le profil général sur le modèle de la voix réelle que je connaissais. Une voix douce, distinguée, un peu lointaine, aimable, pour dire des choses complexes, révolutionnaires, inhabituelles. J'avais été sensible à ce contraste. Je pourrais expliquer cette réceptivité par ma propre histoire psychologique. Je voyais mon père, je l'entendais. Il parlait de cette manière, mais il lui manquait l'autre aspect, cette audace, cette révolte. C'était donc d'abord, pour moi, une voix idéalisée de mon propre père, que j'aimais à retrouver dans un contexte triomphant cette fois. Mais cette impression ne pouvait pas tout expliquer, bien que pour certains ce sera la seule grille de lecture possible. Dans mon esprit elle ne formait qu'un aspect de quelque chose de plus complexe, que j'avais encore peine à expliquer.

Mais Fançois Laruelle (avec son idée de concordance profonde de son écriture avec la composition musicale, avec son intention de composer une sorte d'opéra philosophique) m'encourageait à creuser cette idée de "voix", car je ne pensais pas qu'elle devait se réduire simplement à ce qui resterait de nous, dans les enregistrements que nous pouvions laisser. Il y avait bien plus que cela. C'était la voix de l'autre qui relayait la mienne, cette voix d'acteur, qui, à le lire, jouait mon texte. Comment le lecteur faisait-il résonner dans son esprit, ma voix à moi, sans référence à moi autre que ce que je disais et qui était récurrent, le souffle peut-être...

Ah ! le souffle, on en avait parlé avec Anne-Françoise aussi, une fois qu'on était parti à Zielona Gora, pour une promenade. Quelle est cette idée de souffle? Pour moi, elle semblait avoir été claire, depuis mes études de Victor Hugo *la Fin de Satan*...

Depuis quatre mile ans il tombait dans l'abîme...

Là, je dois dire que le souffle hugolien usait mon souffle à moi, dans cette chute, qui brûlait des centaines d'alexandrins pour se dire. Et mon propre souffle n'arrivait plus à suivre. Je devais reprendre dans une gamme différente pour poursuivre cette chute infinie. Pour l'acteur de ce texte, chargé de le dire, le problème du souffle est vraiment essentiel. Il s'agit de faire tenir l'effet de chute. La voix de Hugo, c'est évidemment cet extraordinaire souffle, qui englobe des centaines de vers dans une même expiration, qui les écrit de ce fait dans une même inspiration. Cette voix qui m'a parlé, usant la mienne, de si longues heures, où je lisais la quasi totalité de son oeuvre, il est absolument certain que tout ce temps elle avait réussi à altérer ma conscience, à la faire entrer dans une sorte de transe hypnotique, au bout de laquelle, moi-même j'improvisais des vers hugoliens, spontanément. Cette voix ne se réduisait pas seulement à son souffle. Elle avait une gamme d'expression. J'étais sensible aux oxymores, qui m'écartelaient à l'extrême, entre ciel et terre comme cette "*bure de mendiant*", devant le feu de bois, qui ressemblait au ciel étoilé quand la lumière traversait ses trous de mites, pour l'observateur, à contre-jour, qui projetait sur lui le sublime de l'ailleurs, le rêve du renversement social, le rêve de la justice céleste, au coeur même des *Contemplations*.

C'était une grande voix de titan que celle de Victor Hugo. J'ai appris à connaître plus tard celle de Nerval. C'est bien une voix de magicien ou de fou inspiré, que cette étrange voix qui hante *les Chimères*. Et c'est encore une voix aimable aussi et toujours inspirée qui nous parle depuis *Aurelia,* au coeur de la folie du narrateur. Toutes ces voix sont bien différentes, et pourtant elles parlent par la mienne. Elles utilisent mon truchement pour s'exprimer. Ces voix d'écrivains sont liées à des personnalités d'artistes, à leur style (comme on dirait pour les arts plastiques), quelque part à leur facture. Et la facture c'est l'originalité. Et l'originalité c'est la spécificité humaine de leur écriture artistique et philosophique. Mais j'ai toujours l'impression que c'est par une voix humaine que tout cela s'exprime. C'est peut-être une illusion d'auditif à la première personne (selon la théorie d'Antoine de La Garanderie), de quelqu'un qui en somme comprend les choses par le code auditif.

C'est un peu une voix que j'ai pu habiller de concepts et d'affects spécifiques, une voix de pantomime, celle d'un personnage invisible, qui vit en moi et me nourrit, sans vraiment disparaître. Et si je réfléchis quelque peu, je suis capable de définir certains de ses critères spécifiques. Ils ne sont pas toujours très évidents à première vue. Mais le souffle, je le perçois très clairement. Il est fait de la rythmique que la voix du passé impose à son discours, qui le traverse et le ponctue. Comme des échos. Lorsque les phrases fusent lentement, elles rejoignent la surface commune de ma présence, où elles se mêlent à ma propre pensée lentement, sans que j'y puisse quelque chose. Et il doit y avoir des voix plus familières pour chacun de nous.

Celle de Nerval est très proche pour moi. Elle chuchote gentiment à mon oreille. Cependant elle est magique, insistante, prophétique, déroutante aussi. Elle est surréaliste avant la lettre et parle dans l'équivoque, comme l'oracle de Delphes. C'est une voix qui a un souffle long. Elle me parle de loin, comme une voix familière et simple, une voix doucement plaintive dans *Aurelia*. Elle concentre en son espace des cristallisations particulières.

Avec François Laruelle, ici, à Kolsko, en Pologne, on était arrivé à même évoquer le timbre de la voix humaine, celui qui pouvait traduire l'essence de chaque être humain en particulier, mais il était difficile de le départir de la voix réelle. Le timbre de la voix réelle de Heidegger nous revient encore par des enregistrements qui nous sont connus maintenant. C'est une voix douce, profilée sur le parler d'un accent rhénan, tel que j'ai pu le connaître pendant les longues années où j'ai vécu à quinze kilomètres de l'Allemagne, dans la plaine d'Alsace, proche, à la fois de Fribourg, et de la Forêt Noire. Dans ma tête qui s'est fait théâtre pour jouer les conférences heideggeriennes, cette voix a certes un timbre différent. Elle a effectivement des caractéristiques propres, mais elles ne sont pas celles qui apparaissent dans les enregistrements de la voix réelle. Elle n'a donc pas les critères objectifs qu'une étude devrait révéler. Et pourtant elle est là, avec son profil précis que je pourrais décrire. Je l'entends dans mon for intérieur.

Qu'est-ce que cela veut dire ? For intérieur ? Tribunal ou scène de théâtre ? Scène de théâtre plutôt, là où se joue l'émotion. C'est cela, c'est de l'émotion, qui faisait que ces voix devenaient humaines, et non robotiques, émotionnellement humaines.

J'avais ressenti de l'émotion dans la connaissance. J'avais compris que je ne pouvais recevoir sans effort que ce qui m'était donné par l'émotion. Et c'est la pensée qui avait cette caractéristique. Une parole humaine forte, exaltée face à l'immensité du monde, et peut-être son vide aussi, une parole héroïque. Et j'avais alors enregistré la voix de Nietzsche, apocalyptique, prophétique, aphoristique, parabolique, allégorique:

> Als Zarathustra dreißig Jahre alt war, verließ er seine Heimat, und der See seiner Heimat, und ging in das Gebirge.

J'avais plongé alors dans une intériorité que je commençai à percevoir comme un refuge de la vie, une sorte de caverne où me parlaient les voix du passé, les voix de la méditation. Et elles avaient un timbre particulier suivant ce qu'elles me disaient. Je les entendais parler, c'était des personnes de mon entourage intérieur. Qu'il fait bon évoquer la douceur de ces instants bénis, où je pouvais retrouver la voix de Balzac, formidable marionnettiste de ses figures, ventriloque royal qui défiait la vie même par la création de son monde. Et je ne l'entendais pas bien cette voix balzacienne, cachée quelle était derrière tant d'autres qui parlaient par sa bouche.

Et je pourrais détailler à l'infini le timbre intérieur de toutes ces voix qui m'ont parlé dans l'émotion, par le souffle de vie que je leur ai accordé, le temps qu'il fallait pour qu'elles puissent me dire ce qu'elles avaient à me dire. Jusqu'à ces voix que j'ai entendues aussi, dont je connaissais à la fois le timbre réel et le timbre virtuel (celui qui parlait dans mon intériorité à moi). Je pense encore tout particulièrement à François Laruelle justement. Je lui disais à Kolsko, combien le choc de ces deux voix était grand, quand j'ai appris à le connaître à Paris, le jour d'un examen de philosophie que j'avais préparé par correspondance. J'avais alors perçu par l'écrit, cette voix laruellienne comme chargée de haute substance volcanique, puissamment émotive et passionnée, même révolutionnaire. Elle avait exalté en moi immédiatement, à la fois un rejet et une profonde fascination. J'étais encore resté un rebelle, un insoumis. Cette voix de Laruelle non-philosophe m'avait appelé directement. Depuis, peut-être par le fait que j'ai surimprimé le timbre agréable de la voix du Laruelle réel sur le Laruelle premier, je n'ai plus ressenti les mêmes choses. Mais je crois aussi, et plus directement, que la voix de Laruelle, sa voix philosophique dans mon esprit, ne pouvait pas se réduire à cette impression première. Au fur et à mesure que je la lisais, qu'elle me parlait donc à travers ce que j'en lisais, j'arrivais à la déterminer avec plus de précision.

C'était une voix de créations conceptuelles, une voix de philosophe. Elle était cryptée. La voix philosophique est toujours cryptée probablement, voilà son apparaître le plus évident. Elle semble avoir été codée dans un langage particulier, dont il faut retrouver les équivalences, les clés. La langue philosophique est programmée de cette manière. La voix philosophique parle donc, à la fois une langue naturelle et une langue apprise. La langue naturelle correspondrait à son caractère propre, à quelque chose de sa personnalité réelle. La langue apprise appartiendrait au domaine qu'elle exprime, comme par exemple la philosophie ou encore la poésie pour le poète. Pour ce qui est de la philosophie (c'est le domaine qui nous intéresse présentement), il s'agit de cerner la langue que cette voix doit apprendre, sans que cela lui soit enseigné directement. C'est une manière d'articuler des concepts inventés ou repensés, de façon cohérente, avant toute exigence à la vérité absolue. Car de fait, depuis Laruelle surtout, mais aussi depuis Deleuze, la philosophie revendique une créativité bien avant de partager de la vérité. La philosophie sort donc de l'esprit de découverte qu'on lui attribuait auparavant, pour entrer dans l'inventivité. Tout cela résonne très fort dans la voix de François Laruelle. Sa voix fait donc sonner ensemble, l'esprit d'inventivité conceptuelle et sa complexe transcription dans le langage philosophique. Je pense qu'il est l'un des plus grands créateurs d'inventivité conceptuelle.

Il reste à présenter clairement cette idée de transcription philosophique, qui est à la base de la langue philosophique. J'ai pu suggérer quelques éléments de ce langage dans certaines paraphrases en allemand sur Heidegger. Il s'agit avant tout d'une opération de cohérence. C'est une mise en cohérence des signes. Les signes étant les unités conceptuelles inventées par le philosophe, comme par exemple dans le langage laruellien, les concepts de "non-philosophie", de "philo-fiction", etc. Ces inventions peuvent aussi reprendre des mots connus *de la tribu,* selon l'expression de Mallarmé, comme "générique", "quantique", "homme ordinaire", etc. C'est la grammaire de l'axe paradigmatique de leur combinaison qui leur accorde un espace philosophique. Pour être plus clair, le discours philosophique est fait d'une écriture qui doit coder les inventions conceptuelles en les inscrivant dans un espace de cohérence, un espace où ils ne heurtent pas l'esprit de vigilance qui vérifie si le propos s'égare en s'étendant. C'est la logique du logos philosophique, que de proposer un espace de cohérence suffisant à l'expansion conceptuelle. Il n'y a pas de place pour l'incohérence, même s'il y a de la place pour une vérité relative.

Mais revenons à notre propos, sur la voix... qu'elle prétende dire ou non la vérité. Dans l'espace de la voix du philosophe, dans la grammaire complexe de sa langue se joue son timbre philosophique, son espace propre, sa voix particulière, composée de concepts, articulée par des lois de cohérence du langage philosophique commun, avec des spécificités hypnotiques particulières. Il faut alors se rappeler que ces spécificités sont justement le fruit de démarches anciennement appelées rhétoriques, que j'appelle non-hypnotiques (de l'espace hypnotique généralisé), dont l'une des fonctions est justement de parler dans un double espace, l'espace commun de référence du lecteur ou de l'auditeur, et l'espace virtuel conceptuel propre au philosophe. Dans la mesure où le lecteur doit accorder une attention accrue et permanente à ce double espace, l'effet de transe philosophique, équivalent de la transe hypnotique ericksonienne, s'en trouve facilité. Et il y a de multiples manières d'activer cette double lecture.

Depuis Heidegger, c'est en fait un jeu de différences, sur lequel se construit le langage de la philosophie, jeu de différences entre la tradition qui transmet le profil habituel du concept que l'on emploie et le concept tel qu'il est utilisé par la voix philosophique nouvelle. Le lecteur doit donc sans cesse faire le passage de l'un à l'autre. Il doit en outre vérifier en permanence la cohérence du nouveau concept dans son nouvel espace. Cette double activité jauge l'espace de cohérence du langage de la voix philosophique. S'il y a des spécificités, elles constituent dans leur ensemble l'équivalent du timbre pour la voix normale. Dans le cas de Heidegger, le passage des concepts du langage courant à ceux du langage propre de la voix philosophique heideggerienne, fait apparaître les mêmes mots sous un autre jour. Ils sont retravaillés, repensés, méconnaissables, tant et si bien que la difficulté de lecture (qui est rappelons-le une lecture de cohérence) est aussi important pour un Allemand que pour un étranger qui pratique la langue allemande. La difficulté est dans le passage incessant d'un code à l'autre. C'est une difficulté, mais c'est également une fascination hypnotique, en partie liée à l'attention qu'elle mobilise pour la lecture de décryptage. Heidegger en prolonge et en renouvelle les structures. Il en tire même parfois des effets, qui provoquent dans l'esprit du lecteur comme un *overflow*, un effet de saturation, qui lui même favorise la transe philosophique. Car c'est bien de cela qu'il s'agit, chaque voix cherche à captiver l'esprit en le déroutant par des concepts, qui lui semblent à première vue familiers, mais qui se révèlent avec l'usage qui en est fait, comme de redoutables concepts au pouvoir de fascination inaccoutumé. Un des plaisirs de lire la philosophie actuelle est dû à ce type de fascination de la voix philosophique et de son langage.

Chaque philosophe laisse en nous la résonance d'une voix. C'est un peu ce que disait Malraux de l'art. Il parlait d'un *musée imaginaire*, qui caractérise chaque artiste. C'est que les artistes parlent tous depuis un musée propre, qu'ils ont constitué en leur for intérieur. De là ils élaborent leur langage, qui soutient leur voix. Mais leur voix c'est ce qu'on appelait leur style et ils décrivent avec lui le monde qui les entoure et qui continuera sans eux, en laissant subsister quelque chose d'eux. Ce musée c'est l'horizon artistique de leur art. Et il y a effectivement un équivalent de ce musée pour la pensée des penseurs, l'horizon verbal ou pictural des romanciers.

Je reviens à mon propos qui cherchait à relever la spécificité de chacune de ces voix, qui nous parle par les livres. Elles sont toutes dans un processus hypnotique de légère transe, conditionné tout premièrement par ce mince filet noir que l'on suit dans le temps et qui représente les lettres de l'alphabet que l'on décrypte en mots et de mots en phrases, pendant que se déroule dans notre esprit un véritable théâtre intérieur, dans lequel nous sommes à la fois présents et absents. Mais plus loin que cette première évidence, il est des textes qui exercent sur nous une fascination plus forte, qui provoquent un état altéré de la conscience beaucoup plus intense que d'autres qui nous bercent dans une douce insouciance. Certainement ces textes ont sur nous un tel pouvoir, parce qu'ils nous parlent dans la direction de ce que nous cherchions nous-même, sans nous en rendre compte clairement. Peut-être jouent-ils avec des éléments qui ont leur double dans notre grenier intérieur, et de ce fait pourraient nous aider à retrouver des routes perdues un peu comme le cheval de Milton Erickson.

Il est tout de même surprenant qu'un texte comme celui de cette conférence de Heidegger sur *l'Origine de la métaphysique* par exemple, nous hypnotise à ce point, que nous pourrions confondre ce qui est dit avec le réel lui-même. Il est une utilisation de la parole conceptuelle qui peut nous pousser à faire de tels efforts à la suivre, que nous pourrions entrer de ce fait dans un état de fascination, qui constituerait le plaisir propre de la voix philosophique en général, mais surtout dès lors où la philosophie a commencé à se présenter comme traduction d'autres textes, derrière lesquelles elle semblait parler. Je pense évidemment à Heidegger, à Derrida, à Deleuze, mais pas tellement à Laruelle. Chez François Laruelle l'articulation n'est plus différentielle, ce n'est plus un texte d'un autre que l'on traduit et paraphrase en y inscrivant subrepticement des mécanismes de pensée nouveaux, qui rendent les mots eux-mêmes étranges et presque méconnaissables, tout en gardant à l'ensemble la même cohérence.

On lit François Laruelle comme une voix qui se traduit elle-même, de neuf à chaque passage mélodique. Et ce n'est pas un leitmotiv, un thème récurrent. C'est une démarche qui procède par cercles concentriques, en spirale peut-être, depuis un motif reçu comme fictif, qui prolifère de manière fractale, en homothétie interne. Le tout dernier Laruelle est de ce fait une voix qui se dit elle-même comme conceptuelle, qui décrit sa naissance, et son parcours dans le monde, qui s'élève dans l'univers. Mais c'est elle qui se dit maintenant, directement, seule peut-être même, comme se détachant de ses anciennes formes, de ses fonctions d'écriture calibrée, et qui se tend et s'étend maintenant comme une musique. Il existe de fait des harmonies, des contrepoints, pour elle dans la musique de ses propres concepts, celle même dont elle retourne à la conscience, la pureté élégante.

Il n'est pas difficile d'en rendre compte par l'exemple. Nous citons un extrait du l'introduction au grand projet de la tétralogie laruellienne, texte non encore publié à cette heure, sur lequel nous avons porté l'attention, lors de l'entrevue culturelle filmée à Kolsko:

> "Un opéra de philosophies" est le titre d'un ensemble de quatre livres ou de quatre actes, d'une tétralogie fondée sur l'affinité philosophico-musicale et dont l'objet général est de décrire, par un montage de théories philosophiques et de références centrales à la musique, l'amplitude harmonique et contrapuntique de l'épopée de la vie humaine en fonction de ses sites qui vont de la Caverne aux Étoiles, la diversité de ses stades et de ses intrigues qui vont de la Naissance à la Messianité. C'est donc une dramaturgie d'esprit philosophique et musical et dont le "livret" est fourni par ce texte et ses "dialogues" philosophico-scientifiques.

On voit clairement que l'entreprise est auto-biographique, et que sa lecture est conceptuelle. Elle utilise deux séries, l'une de la musique, l'autre de l'outillage conceptuel philosophique, pour faire apparaître des harmonies et des contrepoints. Le lecteur est amené à lire en même temps ces deux portées pour les faire consoner. Il est sollicité également, à lire derrière ces partitions, les anciennes mélodies conceptuelles philosophico-scientifiques des ouvrages précédents, dont les plus récentes strates sont le quantique et le générique, qui font également partie de la structure globale, comme des contreforts, des arc-boutants qui soutiennent la cathédrale. L'image vient du texte lui-même ; elle a été développée lors d'un entretien à Kolsko, en Pologne. La nef centrale est la haute nef du transcendantal, où l'être humain fait monter sa voix le long des voûtes vibrantes. On sait que cet être est François lui-même comme voix, avec ce timbre unique dont nous essayons de cerner les spécificités. Les contreforts qui soutiennent la nef centrale, et l'aident à lutter contre la pesanteur naturelle tout en jouant avec elle, retiennent, contiennent magiquement son effondrement, par suite de ses trouées de lumière, de ses vitraux qui fragilisent ses hautes voûtes. Dans cette haute nef sonne la voix de l'homme ordinaire aussi, celui qui se méfie des artefacts et des images. Elle s'appuie sur la contre-pression de l'expérience générique d'un côté, et sur le quantique de l'autre comme dernier développement du scientifique qui a forgé une grande partie de son langage.

Il est sûr que par son épaisseur consonante (*sein Durchklingen*), cette écriture mobilise une attention exceptionnelle, pour un esprit qui doit faire tenir ensemble ce phrasé en apparence divergeant. En lui se retrouvent du ressouvenir, plus que du ressouvenir, de la reminiscence...

> Wie ein Wiederklingen, wenn es nicht ein Widerklingen auch noch scheinen mag...

De fait, disais-je, en parlant comme par la voix de Heidegger en moi, *ce retour de résonance, comme des mélodies qu'on a bien connues, peut être de consonance (Wiederklingen) comme quelque chose qui sonnerait une nouvelle fois comme un écho lointain, ou alors comme une sorte de dissonance calculée (Widerklingen), que la composition conceptuelle nous aurait introduit pour en relever l'harmonie.* Même si je me permets d'introduire de la grammaire heideggerienne dans le propos, je ne veux pas dire que l'écriture de la voix laruelienne soit heideggerienne, loin de là.

> ...Von Vorklingen und Nachklingen wird daher nicht gesprochen, weil es nicht im Vorspiel dieses Denckens sich als Vorkommnis gezeichnet hat...

> On ne parle pas d'un écho (Nachklingen), ni même d'une présonance (Vorklingen), qui pourrait annoncer des mélodies futures non encore exploitées. Le spectacle qui fait apparaître pour la première fois cet accord de pensée, n'en a pas fait un événement en soi.

Je compare également cette musique conceptuelle de Laruelle, au Falstaff de Verdi. Il y a là une profusion de mélodies non encore exploitées qui se lèvent pour un instant, comme des promesses infinies.

> ...Durchklingen scheint mir das traghafte Wort zu sein, die dem schwingenden Konzeptgerüst tiefe Schwingungen und hohe Vibrationen zufügt...

En traduction française par la même voix: *Le mot porteur me paraît être „Durchklingen", cette épaisseur consonante qui apporte à la structure de soutien conceptuelle, d'ondes profondes et de hautes vibrations.*

Et je me rappelle que ce mot de vibration plaisait beaucoup à François Laruelle, pour qui il s'agit de suivre toutes ces vibrations dans leur devenir musique. Nous saisirons alors les harmonies conceptuelles, nous lirons tout cela à la fois. Et la composition dont parlait François Laruelle, sera de philosophie musicale. Mais l'orchestre c'est nous qui le construirons. Il sera d'autant plus riche à l'écoute, que nous aurons le pouvoir de lire et d'interpréter toutes les partitions instrumentales. C'est un peu le défi du sublime que se donne la voix philosophique. Et c'est probablement aussi sa fragilité toute humaine.

... Und es ist schließlich das höchste und zugleich auch das schmächtigste aller Ausdrucksmöglichkeiten, dem Gerüst solche technischen Erfordernisse zuzuschreiben...

Et c'est probablement le point le plus avancé et en même temps le plus fragile qu'une expression de la voix puisse atteindre, que d'inscrire à l'armature conceptuelle, de telles exigences techniques.

Dr. Gilbert Kieffer, International Cultural Center, Kolsko,
gilbert.kieffer[at]gmail.com

BENOÎT MAIRE, ANNE-FRANÇOISE SCHMID (Paris)

Le sens-sans-signe: Pour une éthique de la création

The meaning-without-sign: For an ethics of creation

(Abstract)

The following article is the result of a collaboration between a painter and a woman philosopher. They worked previously on an experimental documentary film about objects and art objects, which was realized at Palais de Tokyo. The painter had illustrated in black and white fictions of philosophy, written during a festival on lost films organized by UNdocumenta in South Korea, and then he made photographs of oil paintings of the English translation. This article about painting and philosophical ethics is their first common text. It aims to show that there is no interdiscipline or passage known between the philosophical work and the painting. The philosopher can not imitate the recognition of the painter nor the painter to repair the philosophical non-encounter. The question then is: What can ethics in this non-symmetrical space? Rather than being a product of philosophy, it is what organizes this space between recognition and non-encounter. It is an ethics for philosophy, rather than the other way around. Ethics force to greet the other philosophers without the grudge of the loss necessary to the invention and allows the painter to know the distances that make him feel the recognition. This ethical space is unknown and can not be covered by the artist's philosophy of access or pre-nomination by indexes. Ethics is this unknown, i.e. it is a sense-without-sign, it is without rules-said but process of indexation and acceptance of the loss.

Keywords: philosophy, ethics, paintings, creativity, invention, meanings

---

Cet article est le fruit d'une collaboration entre un peintre et une philosophe. Ils avaient précédemment travaillé sur un documentaire expérimental sur les objets et les objets d'art tourné au Palais de Tokyo, le peintre avait illustré, tout d'abord en noir et blanc, des fictions de la philosophie, écrites à l'occasion d'un festival sur les films perdus organisé par UNdocumenta en Corée du sud, puis par des photographies de peintures à l'huile la traduction anglaise. Cet écrit sur la peinture et l'éthique philosophique est leur premier texte commun.

Structure de l'article :

1) L'impossible rencontre des philosophies
2) Comment reconnaître une peinture ?
3) Une nouvelle philosophie perd d'autres philosophies
4) Toute peinture est une peinture de nuages
5) La philosophie comme un "X"
6) Le paradigme conceptuel comme anecdote de la peinture du 21ème siècle
7) Usage autonyme des philosophies dans une autre
8) Le sens sans signe
9) Conclusion

1. L'impossible rencontre des philosophies

En 1647, Descartes rencontre Pascal à Paris, en 1676, Leibniz vient trouver Spinoza à Amsterdam, le 22 mars 1911, Bergson et Russell déjeunent ensemble au restaurant, alors que Russell venait donner des conférences à Paris. Ces rencontres ont quelque chose de commun, c'est que rien n'en a filtré. Or, ce n'est pas anecdotique, deux philosophes créateurs ne peuvent se comprendre, cela est un trait constant et spécifique de la philosophie. Il y a un "secret ouvert" d'une philosophie, et le cogito du philosophe reste obscur, en ce qu'il ne peut comprendre toute philosophie. À cette incompréhension peut être jaugé le "contemporain", en effet les philosophies semblent ne se comprendre ou se comparer que lorsqu'elles se donnent dans un cadre historique.

2. Comment reconnaître une peinture ?

Considérons trois peintures reconnues telles. Un saint Sébastien transpercé de flèches du *quattrocento* de Mantegna, une peinture pré-cubiste de Cézanne du 19ème représentant une pomme sur une table, et un monochrome blanc plus récent de Robert Ryman. Déjà ces trois peintures ont un auteur, elles sont l'œuvre d'un peintre. Mais ce peintre les a-t-il seulement peintes ? Il est clair que le bon sens consiste à dire, que c'est bien Cézanne qui a peint cette pomme sur une table, de même pour Mantegna (même si à l'époque, on peut présumer que la toile étant un travail d'atelier certains apprentis ont dû exécuter des parties de la composition), et c'est encore le cas pour Ryman. Ces peintures sont rattachées à un peintre, elles ont un titre et existent dans le corpus peint d'un peintre. Mais ici, on tient à dire que ces trois peintres sont seulement les opérateurs de peintures qui arrive d'elles-mêmes à partir de certaines conditions posées par les artistes. Les peintures arrivent, et les trois peintres les reconnaissent comme des peintures. Ils les reconnaissent en premier, et c'est ce qui les autorise à en être dit l'auteur. Ces trois artistes sont dits peintres pour la raison qu'en fonction de certaines conditions qu'ils mettent en place (toile enduite, qualité d'une huile, colle de peau de lapin, tension, agrafes, cyan en pigment pur, magenta, brun Van Dick, humidité de l'air, glacis, temps, mouvement) certaines peintures arrivent. Leur rôle en tant que peintre est essentiellement de reconnaître des peintures, et de les reconnaître en premier. Leur rôle est de reconnaître en premier, des choses qui arrivent (en partie à cause de certaines conditions qu'ils ont organisées) et qui sont des peintures. Cela signifie qu'ils engagent dès lors qu'ils ont reconnu en premier une peinture d'autres à la reconnaître comme telle. Et en général force est de constater que celles qu'ils reconnaissent sont reconnues telles ensuite par le circuit de l'art, qui est un circuit d'intégration (ce qui rejoint en partie la position de George Dickie[1]). La première chose à noter est donc ce caractère ontologique général, que la peinture bien que créée par le peintre est une sorte d'être qui arrive, qui relève d'un type d'*il y a* et qui se détache de l'être du peintre, comme étant une peinture. Peut-on dire que la peinture créée par le peintre est une manifestation du peintre ? Une expression ? Peut-être, mais dans ce texte, on voudrait avancer l'hypothèse que toute peinture est une peinture de nuages. À partir de cette égalité généralisée à toutes peintures : quelle que soit une peinture = une peinture de nuages.

3. Une nouvelle philosophie perd d'autres philosophies

Il y a un paradoxe propre à la philosophie. Lorsqu'un philosophe élabore une philosophie, lorsqu'il devient philosophe, il perd les autres philosophies, leurs particularités deviennent comme des icônes ou des portraits de philosophies, "je suis leibnizien", "je suis kantien", "je suis sartrien". Lorsque l'on passe d'une icône à l'autre, le moment philosophique de vérité n'est pas dans l'une ou l'autre, mais juste dans l'instantané du passage de l'une à l'autre, et c'est la capacité à identifier ce passage sans icône et sans narration qui fait accéder à la philosophie. Une philosophie se crée comme critique, comme correction ou dépassement

---

[1] La théorie dite "institutionnelle" de George Dickie, consiste à définir l'ontologie de l'œuvre par la reconnaissance d'un milieu autorisé à légiférer sur l'être des œuvres d'art. Un objet s'institue œuvre d'art car il est reconnu tel par une communauté faisant autorité en la matière. Ontologie faible des objets d'arts qui sont liés à l'institution validant leur statut et qui ne sont pas considérés en-soi mais en relation à une autorité ponctuelle (cf. Dickie 1974, Beardsley 1976, Yanal 1994).

d'une opinion ou d'une posture extraite d'une autre philosophie. Elle s'avance en en excluant d'autres, elle fait des alliances en perdant d'autres philosophies.

4. Toute peinture est une peinture de "nuages"

Il est donc important de considérer qu'une peinture de Cézanne représentant une pomme sur une table, une peinture de Mantegna représentant un Saint-Sébastien traversé de flèches, ou encore une toile blanche de Ryman sont des peintures de "nuages" (cf. Damisch 1992; Maire 2017). Ainsi, bien qu'aucune de ces peintures n'affirment le nuage comme son sujet, d'un point de vue ontologique elles sont "nuageuses". Il y a là l'apparence d'un forçage, mais seulement l'apparence, car l'identité proposée pour être valide doit se comprendre à une autre distance du point de vue. Souvent quand on regarde une peinture on se place à un mètre d'elle ou un peu plus en fonction de sa taille. En fait on se place à la bonne distance de l'iconicité. Mais n'avez-vous jamais vu un peintre regarder une peinture ? Il la regarde de très près car il veut savoir s'il est second dans la reconnaissance de l'arrivée d'une peinture et ne va pas accepter la distance de l'iconicité.

De plus il se place au-delà de l'institution légitimante qui dit dans le musée ou la galerie "attention il y a là une peinture, c'est certifié !" — ce qui a pour défaut de n'autoriser personne à les reconnaître en second. Lui, le peintre, vient poser son œil bien plus proche, il vient voir les détails de matière et la touche du peintre et il regarde là où il ne voit pas le motif, car il est bien attiré par autre chose : le nuage. Alors, il ne s'agit pas de dire que la pomme rouge de Cézanne serait une sorte de nuage flamboyant et que la table serait une autre sorte de nuage un peu brun, et que l'espace autour seraient des nuages vaporeux. Il s'agirait dans le cas de la reconnaissance en second de ne pas reconnaître l'iconicité de la représentation "pomme sur table", tout simplement par ce que l'on vient reconnaître la peinture selon la modalité d'une autre distance. Que Mantegna soit l'obligé d'une certaine iconicité religieuse, que Cézanne soit l'obligé de la figuration, même réduite au vestige pauvre de la nature morte et que Ryman soit l'obligé du primat moderniste de la surface *all over*, sont des particularités historiques. L'iconicité de leur travail est historique, contextuelle, liée à une époque donnée, on oserait dire que cette iconicité, le sens visuel et signifiant de ces peintures, est anecdotique. Ainsi le caractère ontologique de ces peintures est ailleurs, en dehors de leur sens signifié et à concevoir par l'exercice d'une autre distance.

5. La philosophie comme un "X"

Ce paradoxe nous conduit à traiter la philosophie comme un "X", comme un phénomène qui n'est pas connu complètement. On ne peut la comprendre en faisant une liste de ses auteurs, Platon, montrant le Ciel et Aristote la Terre, ce serait un savoir comme formé de l'extérieur, d'une objectivité historique et non philosophique. Cette liste, c'est pourtant ce que font les philosophes, quand ils se voient d'une lignée plutôt platonicienne (le "X" de la dignité) ou plutôt aristotélicienne (la dignité de chaque "X"). Et pourtant le Ciel et la Terre sont comme les horizons de la philosophie.

6. Le paradigme conceptuel comme anecdote de la peinture du 21ème siècle

Au début du 21ème siècle, début bien entamé car nous sommes au présent de l'écriture de ce texte en 2017, le paradigme anecdotique contemporain majeur est celui qui se rapporte à l'énoncé conceptuel. L'art de la peinture contemporaine, sauf à qualifier ce qui se fait de particulièrement pompier – et qui sera porté hors de l'inscription historique –, est conceptuel. Ryman n'était pas conceptuel, ni Cézanne, ni Mantegna. Ce qui fait une peinture conceptuelle c'est encore un rapport à l'iconicité, pas à la peinture. Il ne faut pas se méprendre et croire que je disqualifie l'iconicité, non, c'est une couche nécessaire, mais ce n'est pas dans l'iconicité que réside l'être de la peinture, c'est dans son expression non-signifiante. Cette expression non-signifiante, *sens-sans-signe* est reconnue en premier par le peintre, et la reconnaissance de cette arrivée permet à la peinture d'être sauvée et présenté à un tiers, le modèle d'un circuit d'intégration. C'est important qu'un peintre sache finir une peinture même sans savoir pourquoi. On peut considérer que la finir c'est la reconnaître dans son être comme une peinture arrivée. Qu'une peinture soit bonne ou mauvaise relève d'une autre question, celle d'un jugement qualitatif, mais qu'une peinture en soit une, relève d'un jugement ontologique. Ainsi le peintre peut aimer certaines peintures moins que d'autres, et par conséquent en déduire que certaines sont meilleures que d'autres, mais cela n'enlève pas le statut ontologique d'être une peinture à celles qui sont le moins aimées. Nous voyons ainsi pourquoi j'ai d'abord fait des peintures de nuages. J'ai fait des peintures de nuages pour reconnaître que ce qui m'arrivait dans l'atelier était des peintures. Je ne savais pas encore les reconnaître, alors cette stratégie conceptuelle posant une identité me permettait de reconnaître mes peintures de nuages comme des peintures arrivées, car une peinture est toujours une peinture de nuages selon l'identité conceptuelle que j'avais posée. Mais au fil du temps, devenant peintre comme je l'avais déjà été entre 1996 et 2002, période où j'ai fait de nombreuses peintures, j'ai su reconnaître mes peintures autrement que conceptuellement. Vous me diriez : Ainsi pourquoi ne pas avoir peint autre chose que des nuages dans ce cas ? Puisque vous saviez dès lors reconnaître une peinture sans avoir à la qualifier conceptuellement comme étant une peinture ? Je crois qu'en continuant à faire des peintures de nuages, je faisais des peintures doubles, chaque peinture était deux fois une peinture, reconnue conceptuellement (par son iconicité conceptuelle) et aussi autrement, par cette façon que l'on ne sait dire quand on se place à la bonne distance.

7. Usage autonyme des philosophies dans une autre

Entre ces limites, le philosophe fait un usage autonyme d'autres philosophies dans la sienne, et sans ce geste il n'y aurait que des œuvres philosophiques isolées. Un usage autonyme prend comme la chose même, la philosophie de l'autre, dans son propre discours. L'autre philosophe parle alors en lui, comme s'il avait transformé sa voix et sa musique en un contrepoint, mais "sans" rencontre. Dans ce "sans", on reconnaît quelque chose de la philosophie qui échappe à l'icône, un principe de générosité – c'est l'ouverture, on peut passer d'une philosophie à l'autre –, et un principe de non-exclusion – c'est le secret de la négation contre la perte, il y a une multiplicité de droit des philosophies, invisible dans les listes ou les séries. L'éthique pour la philosophie consiste à manifester dans ce secret ouvert la multiplicité de droit et la générosité, donc à ne plus être tout-à-fait dans la philosophie, mais hors d'elle, avec elle. C'est une éthique pour un nouveau style philosophique.

8. Le sens sans signe

Ryman, Mantegna et Cézanne ne se sont pas rencontrés, mais tout peintre ou spectateur du 21ème siècle a vu leurs peintures. Leurs peintures se sont rencontrées dès lors dans l'appréciation de tout spectateur. Les peintures de Ryman, Mantegna et Cézanne, et ce sont des exemples absolument pris au hasard, se rencontrent en se composant aussi dans la plupart des peintures contemporaines. Mais quelle est la qualité de cette rencontre ? Les peintures passées, arrivées, se mélangent dans les peintures suivantes, dans les nouvelles peintures qui arrivent, selon une modalité particulière. L'éthique est ici la rencontre de l'incommensurabilité de l'arrivée, c'est un ciel composé de nuages. Ce ciel, plan de rencontres, est vide, c'est un zéro, et ce qui s'y manifeste n'est pas stable, lieu de prise de forme en continuel changement. Ce qui se fixe dans ce ciel, lieux de formations des nuages, n'est pas non plus l'iconicité, que l'on a défini comme un plan de vision dépendant d'une certaine distance de la perception. Ce qui se fige dans ce ciel est désigné par un doigt, c'est un enfant qui pointe du doigt un nuage, c'est un adulte qui dit à un ami regarde là, c'est telle forme, etc... Les nuages figés sont des nuages indexés, ils ne sont pas dits, mais montrés du doigt, ils sont antérieurs à l'accès à la nomination, les nuages comme les peintures, sont pré-dits. Alors les peintures sont dites par indexation, à la condition de l'impossible de leur nomination. Puis les regards se croisent après avoir vu l'innommable, et dans les yeux qui se rejoignent après avoir vu une peinture non-dite, on voit un nouveau ciel, un nouveau lieu de prise de formes et de fantasmes. Le vide perçu dans la jointure de ces yeux est la condition éthique de la composition d'une rencontre non dite celle d'une autre peinture sans-signe.

9. Conclusion

Il n'y a pas d'interdiscipline ou de passage donné ou connu entre l'œuvre philosophique et la peinture. Le philosophe ne saurait imiter la reconnaissance du peintre ni le peintre réparer la non-rencontre philosophique. Qu'est-ce que peut l'éthique dans cet espace non symétrique ? Plutôt qu'être un produit de la philosophie, elle est ce qui organise cet espace entre la reconnaissance et la non-rencontre. Elle est une éthique pour la philosophie, plutôt que l'inverse. L'éthique force à saluer les autres philosophes sans la rancune de la perte nécessaire à l'invention et permet au peintre de savoir les distances qui lui font éprouver la reconnaissance. Cet espace éthique est inconnu, ne pouvant être recouvert par la philosophie de l'accès ou la pré-nomination par indexes de l'artiste. C'est cet inconnu qui est l'éthique : *sens-sans-signe*. Se dérobe alors à l'éthique le traitement moral de situations données, car elle est sans règles-dites mais processus d'indexation et acceptation de la perte.

Benoit Maire, M.A., Palais de Tokyo, contact[at]benoitmaire.com
Prof. Dr. Anne-Françoise Schmid, MINES ParisTech, annefschmid@gmail.com

Références

Beardsley, Monroe. "Is art essentially institutional ?", in Aagaard-Morgensen, Lars (éd.). *Culture and Art*. Atlantic Highlands: Humanities Press, 1976. 194-209.

Damish, Hubert. *Théorie du nuage. Pour une histoire de la peinture*. Paris: Seuil, 1992.

Dickie, George. *Art and the Aesthetic. An Institutional Analysis*. Ithaca: Cornell University Press, 1974.

Maire, Benoît. "Philosophy and Art", *Aleï Journal* #2 (2017): 166-174.

Yanal, Robert J. *Institutions of Art. Reconsiderations of George Dickie's Philosophy*. University Park: Pennsylvania State Univiversity Press, 1994.

www.ingramcontent.com/pod-product-compliance
Lightning Source LLC
Chambersburg PA
CBHW081332230426
43667CB00018B/2905